The Mystery Fancier

2.50

July·Aug '83

The Mystery Fancier

Volume 7, Number 4
July/August 1983

TABLE OF CONTENTS

MYSTERIOUSLY SPEAKING	Page 1
The Complexity of **The Nine Tailors** By Joe R. Christopher	Page 3
Spy Series Characters in Hardback, Part XIV By Barry Van Tilburg	Page 10
Lady Molly of Scotland Yard By Earl F. Bargainnier	Page 15
IT'S ABOUT CRIME By Marvin Lachman	Page 20
REEL MURDERS Movie Reviews by Walter Albert	Page 24
VERDICTS Book Reviews	Page 27
THE DOCUMENTS IN THE CASE Letters	Page 35

The Mystery Fancier
(USPS:428-590)
is edited and published bi-monthly by
Guy M. Townsend
1711 Clifty Drive
Madison, IN 47250

SUBSCRIPTION RATES: Second-class mail, U.S. and Canada, $12.00 per year (6 issues); first-class mail, U.S. and Canada, $15.00; overseas surface mail, $12.00; overseas air mail, $18.00. Overseas subscribers please pay in international money order, check drawn on U.S. bank, or currency; no checks drawn on foreign banks, please.

Single copy price: $2.50
Second-class postage paid at Madison, Indiana
Copyright 1982 by Guy M. Townsend
All rights reserved for contributors
ISSN:0146-3160

First, my embarrassed apologies for the extreme lateness of this issue. I have an excuse--a damned good one--but you wouldn't believe it (sometimes I don't myself), so I'll just let it go with a simple apology and a promise to try to do better.

I received forty-four responses to my query about raising the subscription rate by $3.00 to pay contributors. There were eight negative responses (ranging from one or two flat nays to a couple from the "well, I don't know ..." school. The rest all supported the increase, although a few suggested that I raise the rates but put the increased revenue in my pocket rather than use it to pay contributors, a temptation which **I think** I'm going to be able to resist. Encouragingly, no one wrote to state flatly that he or she would not renew if I increased the price. But, then, three hundred of you did not write at all.... Even so, I'm going to take the four-to-one vote as an endorsement of the increase, and volume eight will cost you three bucks more than the current one.

As some of you have suggested, and as I myself have pointed out, half a cent per ain't much. Assuming that most of you stay with me despite the price increase, there should be a little money left in the kitty after the contributors have been paid, and I have an idea--the germ of which was contributed by Paulette Greene--about how that money might be employed. Bear in mind now that what I am proposing would be **in addition to** rather than instead of payment of individual contributors. Here it is: what would you folks think about awarding a substantial (?) cash prize--say a hundred bucks--to the contributor who does the most for TMF each year? We'll have to work out the details later--such as who would be eligible, what form the voting should take, etc.--but right now I'd just like to have your reactions to the idea. If we did it, then in addition to the pittance they would receive for each piece they had published, contributors would stand a chance of picking up a little extra at year's end--not to mention the ego-boost that would come from being named MFer of the year. (Let it lie, Texans, let it lie.) Let me know your feelings on this.

Lots of other stuff to cover in this limited space. Scribners Crime Classics paperback line is still going strong. Most recently received are Robert van Gulik's Judge Dee mystery, **The Haunted Monastery** ($2.95) and two Philo Vance Murder Cases--**Benson** and **Bishop** (both $3.95). I'll forgive Scribners for a lot of minor sins because they have retained the superb period covers from the old Fawcett reprints of these two Van Dine books; I don't often get excited about covers, but there's something about these that I find incredibly appealing (though God only knows whether I'd be able to wade through a Philo Vance novel nowadays ...).

My favorite cataloguer, Enola Stewart, has done it again, although I'm rather late in mentioning it. Catalogue 28 is available from Gravesend Books, Box 235, Pocono Pines, PA 18350, for $5.00. If you are a regular customer, you get it free. Most of the items are annotated, so it, like all of Enola's catalogues, is an excellent reference work as well.

Two more catalogues you should know about are #13 from Keith & Martin Bookshop, 310 W. Franklin St., Chapel Hill, NC 27514 (said shop being run pseudonymously by the infamous Bill Loeser), and #14 from Post Mortem Books, 5 Standford Ave., Hassocks, Sussex BN6 8JL, ENGLAND. The second also contains several pages pleasant chatter.

The latest specialist fanzine to hit the streets is **The 87th Precinct Report**, devoted, though you don't need to be told this, to Ed McBain's procedural series of the same number. The first issue runs to six pages and is in the form of--you guessed it--a police report. Membership in The 87th Precinct Squadroom, which includes a subscription to the quarterly newsletter, is $4.00 in the U.S., $5.00 in Canada, and $6.00 anywhere else. Write to The 87th Precinct Squadroom, Russell Hultgren, Lieutenant, Apartment 12, 701 Dondee Dr., Manhattan, KS 66502.

Here's something I really shouldn't tell you about, since there is virtually no chance you will be able to get a copy if you don't already have one--Joe R. Christopher has published a 36-page chapbook entitled **Queen's Books Investigated: Or, Queen is in the Accounting House**, including eight of Joe's articles on Ellery Queen which have previously appeared in either **The Queen Canon Bibliophile** or **The Armchair Detective**. Why shouldn't you be able to get a copy? Let me quote from the last page: "This chapbook is published in July 1983 (less than a year after Frederic Dannay's death) in an edition of thirty copies, none offered for sale, for the amusement and possible edification of some of the author's friends and acquaintances and for a few detective fans who seem to need a copy." I was one of the lucky ones.

Mike Nevins is hard at work giving a new meaning to the word ubiquitous. Besides doing the latest release from Brownstone Books and the introductions to the many Woolrich paperback releases, he has, with Martin H. Greenberg, just turned out two collections of short stories, and had written the introduction for one of them. The one he did the introduction for is **Exeunt Murderers: The Best Mystery Stories of Anthony Boucher** (326 pp., $16.95), and the other, with an introduction by Bob Briney, is **Buffet for Unwelcome Guests: The Best Short Mysteries of Christianna Brand** (316 pp., $16.95). Both are published by Southern Illinois University Press, P.O. Box 3697, Carbondale, IL 62901.

This last item probably will be news to no one, but **The Saint Magazine** is about to be reborn (if it hasn't been already by the time you receive this). This is good news for readers of short mystery fiction, since there are so damned few places to buy the stuff nowadays, and even better news for writers of short mystery fiction, since there are so damned few places to sell the stuff nowadays. Look for it on your newsstand, and if you've got an unpublished manuscript on hand why not send it off to editor Keith Bancroft, P.O. Box 8468, Van Nuys, CA 91409. To the best of my knowledge, none of the existing mystery magazines pays nearly as well as **The Saint**.

The Complexity of The Nine Tailors

Joe R. Christopher

A paper read in
the Christianity and Literature Special Session
of the South Central Modern Language Association Meeting
in San Antonio, Texas, 29 October 1982.

In a 1937 essay, Dorothy L. Sayers comments on her 1934 mystery novel, **The Nine Tailors,** saying that it "was a shot at combining detective with poetic romance, and was, I think, pretty nearly right." She goes on to speak of some weaknesses in the book, but I am interested in her terming **The Nine Tailors** a "poetic romance." What could she mean by it? She does not explain, and she may not have had a precise meaning in mind.

But I find the book a complex novel, certainly if compared to the average mystery; and this complexity, if not quite the same thing as being poetry or a romance in itself, at least allows for different sorts of interpretations, or critical approaches to the work, as I assume are characteristic of readers' reactions to such poetic romances as Spenser's **Faerie Queene** or Chaucer's **Knight's Tale.** I find five, or perhaps six, such approaches to **The Nine Tailors.**

I begin with the most obvious level: the book is a mystery novel. Lord Peter Wimsey is Sayers' most often used sleuth, appearing in eleven novels, twenty-one short stories, and one play. Here he solves three interrelated mysteries: first, whose body is it that was buried, shallowly, in Lady Thorpe's grave, and why was it buried there; second, what is the meaning of an obscure message--"I thought to see fairies in the fields, but I saw only the evil elephants with their black backs," etc.--found by Hilary Thorpe in the bell tower of the church at Fenchurch St. Paul; and third, what happened to the jewels which were stolen by a servant from a guest when Hilary's grandfather was lord of the manor--of the Red House, as it is called--in that same village in the fen country of England.

Since this is one of those elaborate puzzle mysteries which were written during what is called the Golden Age between the World Wars, it is not surprising that the message turns out to be an elaborate cipher, drawn up by the villain for purposes of convincing another criminal to join him in an enterprise. When the message is arranged in columns of eight letters each, punctuation and spaces omitted, and when the pattern of one particular bell in a certain method of English change-ringing of church bells is traced throughout, then three quotations from the Psalms are discovered. These three passages, properly interpreted--and one involves a pun--tell where the missing jewels are hidden. O, most rare villains of the time, who made, most precisely, messages too elaborate for their fellow criminals to interpret! And how marvelous that such messages had to be dropped, as clues, in the room in which a man was killed, only to be found by an innocent person who hands it to the detective (or in this case mails it to him) about mid-point in the novel.

What I suggest, of course, is that the Golden Age mystery was an elaborate artifice. Sayers struggled to add interest to the form, with humor in the early novels and characterizations in the later; but she also observed the generic demands. What I find interesting about this particular novel is how much chance determines the workings of the plot. With the cipher, for instance: there was no need for Geoffrey Deacon to work out a real cipher. Nobby Cranton decides to help him recover the jewels without understanding the cipher, although he asked for it as evidence of trust--so that Deacon would not double-cross him as he had once before. (It's also amazing that Deacon remembered the pattern of the bells for about fifteen years, during which he's lived in France, away from the English practice of ringing changes.)

Moreover, it is chance that Cranton drops the cipher when he visits the bell-chamber, by chance, on the evening after Deacon had died there (while the body is still there). It is also chance that Hilary Thorpe finds the cipher, although that one does not matter so much, as **someone** would have found it anyway.

Finally, it is chance that Lord Peter interprets the cipher. He happens to have it arranged in columns of eight letters each when the Rector brings in a hot toddy and a foot-warmer one evening. Mr. Venables (we'd say the Reverend Venables) nearsightedly thinks Wimsey is working out bell changes. At that point Lord Peter considers tracing a bell's pattern in his columns. (I also consider it remarkable that Lord Peter wrote out the whole of the message in columns of eight when no message began to appear in the first part, down some column; but perhaps he is a methodical man, thinking it might appear only near the end.)

I could do the same thing with Lord Peter's discovery of the solution of the murder--chance drives him to the bell-tower at an appropriate time--but I think the pattern is clear enough. I will return to this pattern of chance later in my discussion with another explanation.

Next, I would like to turn to the novel as a regional fiction, as parallel to the local-color stories in late nineteenth-century America. Of course, in England the great model--one who turned regional fiction into universal fiction--is Thomas Hardy; and several critics, particularly Sara Lee Soloway in her 1971 dissertation, have drawn parallels between Hardy and Sayers. It may be true that there are resemblances between the peasants of nineteenth-century Wessex and early twentieth-century East Anglia. Critics are divided in their appreciation of the ringing of bell changes in the novel, Edmund Wilson, at the most extreme, denouncing the material on it as a sort of treatise on campanalogy; James Burleson, in his 1965 dissertation, attempted an answer of Wilson in terms of its necessity to the plot. I would observe only that one hardly learns enough to work a course of Grandsire Triples or Kent Treble Bob Major on one's own; there **is** a lot of terminology from the practice in the book, but this is what one expects from a local-color tory.

I do not want to spend much time on the other regional aspects, but critics have praised the description of the fen country--as well as damned it. But those who have damned it, like Ralph Partridge, a reviewer, have tended to be those who complain not of the realism but the amount of time spent on description and conversation between local inhabitants as taking away from the detective plot. Edmund Wilson, after all, thought the whole thing should have been a short story.

Likewise, the characterization of the local personages has been praised by some and denounced by others. Wilson, for example, complained of all the dialect. (What he would have said about **The Five Red Herrings,** Sayers' Scottish novel, I can't imagine.) Others have spent time on the various local characters. Certainly Burleson in his dissertation does, and Sister Mary Brian Durkin in her 1980 book on Sayers, despite the cramped format of The Twayne English Authors Series, spends a paragraph each on Mr. Venables and Potty Peake--the latter the simpleton of the village. My point is not so much the critical controversy, although that has its liveliness, as the fact that some readers do find pleasure in the regional aspects of the book.

However, what is mostly done with the local color of this story is to tie it with Sayers' own background: a childhood in the fen country, with her own father an Anglican priest. Most of the conjectures on this, which I may label the third approach, have been laid to rest by James Brabazon's 1981 authorized biography of Sayers. For example, he says that Mr. Venables is like the Reverend Sayers in his willingness to go to the aid of his parishioners at any time of the day or night and in his gentle scholarliness; but he is unlike Henry Sayers in his fussiness and comic behavior, which come from stage clergymen. And, indeed, isn't this blending of autobiography and other materials what we often find in novels? In Sayers' case, since she is writing a popular novel, she blends her memories of her father with some conventional depiction of clerics to produce what is neither a simple joke nor straight biography. Oddly enough, Brabazon says nothing about Mrs. Venables, so her relationship with Mrs. Sayers--with Dorothy L. Sayers' mother--is still a matter of conjecture. Brabazon does report that some of the parishioners in Henry Sayers' second church in the fen country insist that some of Sayers' minor characters are taken from life. Whether they really were, or Sayers just got the types so well down that readers of the area make their own applications, I do not know.

Another matter which has created an autobiographical question relates to the Reverend Sayers and ringing of bell-changes. Janet Hitchman, in her 1975 biography of Sayers--the first biography published--said that his parish church had no bells. But she seems to have seen the second parish of which Henry Sayers was rector, for Ralph Hone, in his later, 1979 book, reports that the first parish has a set of eight bells like the invented church in the novel, with one of the eight given by the Reverend Sayers and his Senior Warden. Thus Dorothy L. Sayers presumably heard change-ringing as a child, although she has said in a published letter that she had to work up the details for the book, never having seen the actual ringing of the bells when she wrote it.

A final autobiographical element in the novel, which only Ralph Hone seems to have noticed, is Hilary Thorpe. She is something of a portrait of Sayers at an early age, although given red hair and greater beauty, and with a gentry background substituted for the clerical. Hilary tells her father she wants to be a a popular novelist, not a poet, because poetry doesn't pay; Sayers, after publishing two books of poetry early in her career, came to the same conclusion. Hilary has a teacher she idolizes at school--a Miss Bowler, the English mistress; Sayers, at the private school she attended for a few years, had the same feeling for Miss White, who taught French. Hilary wants to go on to Oxford; and, after her father's death and some complications about her inheritance, Lord Peter Wimsey works out the details with her uncle, who is her guardian; Sayers, of course, was born in Oxford, attended Somerville College there, and was in the first group of women to receive degrees from the University. Hilary has a poor view of the intelligence of most of the girls at her school; Sayers never throughout her life suffered fools gladly--despite the fact that she has Lord Peter tell Hilary that it's not kind to tell her schoolmates of their inferiority. (This is not the same thing as saying they are her equals in intelligence!) Although not precisely the same type of parallel, Hilary reports that her father disapproved of tombstones and did not plan to put one on his wife's grave, Sayers put no tombstones on the graves of her parents.

I put forward these parallels not as making **The Nine Tailors** a **roman a clef**, but simply as one of the increased densities--so to speak--of the book. It is not unusual for novelists to use their private or public backgrounds in their books. Sayers used the area of London she lived in as a young adult--Bloomsbury--in several of the early Wimsey novels; she used the area of Scotland that she and her husband vacationed in for **The Five Red Herrings**; she used her nine years of work in an advertising agency for **Murder Must Advertise**; she used Somerville College, Oxford, for background in **Gaudy Night**. I think it is the affection shown for Mr. Venables in this book which gives it some of its autobiographical interest. Sayers' father died in 1928; and, after about two years of work on it, this novel appeared in 1934. This dimension is technically extra-literary, but few knowledgeable readers will neglect it.

Fourth, I turn to the Gothic side of the book. It is appropriate that among the authors providing epigraphs for chapters--mainly books on change-ringing and books from the Old Testament--are Edgar Allan Poe and Sheridan LeFanu. Sayers also has an epigraph from a Gothic short story by Julian Sermet, "The Rosamund," which two characters in the novel previously mention in passing. But she may have made that one up, for I have been unable to trace any such author. If she made it up, this was probably because she needed a passage in which a bell killed a person: it's certainly appropriate for her book.

In the novel the Gothic note is struck--by the bells. I count seven passages in the book in which the bells are referred to as alive, as dangerous, as frightening. Mrs. Venables makes such a comment in passing to Lord Peter when she is showing him around the church. When Hilary Thorpe accompanies Jack Godfrey up to the bell-chamber while he is greasing and oiling the mechanism, he refuses to let her approach one of the bells, explaining that it--a bell cast back in medieval times--has killed two men through the ages, striking one who was in the bell-chamber (one of Cromwell's men, come to desecrate the church) and hanging another who got tangled in the ropes. He also claims it rang all night, without a hand to it, when the monks were turned out of the abbey by Henry VIII. Still later, when Lord Peter first climbs into the bell-chamber, he feels the bells' presence as depression and vertigo. Nobby Cranton twice tells of the effect of the bells on him--the second time adding that he thought one of them was alive. Jim Thoday also reports this type of feeling, although he was admittedly removing Geoffrey Deacon's dead body at the time, and that may have made him nervous.

All of these are preparation for the fact that Deacon was tied up in the bell-chamber during the nine-hour ringing of bell-changes on New Year's Eve and early morning. He presumably died of a stroke or something like that during the period. That Sayers does not define what he died of, and does not give him a weak heart or any of the other conventional means of dying used in detective fiction, suggests that she wants to leave the matter open to a Gothic reading in which the bells killed him mysteriously. Jacques Barzun in his comments on this book has complained on this as a weak denouement of the mystery; but he is working at the level of the detective-story plot, and he fails to see the Gothic level which is also important.

For the fifth approach, I turn to one which is especially appropriate for this meeting. The novel is also open to a Christian interpretation throughout—and, in fact, Mr. Venables offers it. When Lord Peter has his car accident at the first of the book and turns up at Fenchurch St. Paul, the rector four times says that his coming is providential, since he, with his experience, can replace one of the bell-ringers who is ill. He says it twice to Mrs. Venables and Lord Peter, once to the bell-ringers assembled for practice and handbells, and once in his New Year's Eve sermon. At this point Mr. Venables' interpretation is limited, since the bell ringing will kill Geoffrey Deacon, but it sets the motif.

Sayers stresses the theme of providence in a humorous manner later in the book when Mr. Venables is visiting an old woman of his flock. She picks up the word as he uses it and denounces providence: "Don't you talk to me about Providence. I've had enough of Providence. First he took my husband, and then he took my taters, but there's One above as'll teach him to mind his manners, if he don't look out." This, if nothing else, should make the reader remember the theme.

Before I reach the final passage on this theme, I want to pause over two matters. First, I see Lord Peter as essentially a foil to the rector in this matter of belief. This is in contrast to the detective story where Wimsey is the protagonist, of course. At the burial of Geoffrey Deacon's body, Lord Peter muses on a passage about the resurrection of the body: "Do all these people believe that? Do I? Does anybody? We all take it pretty placidly, don't we?" Wimsey as a decorous but essentially secular modern individual is placed in contrast to the rector's faith, and also (more implicitly) the faith of the congregation. Mary Thoday, for example, is a regular communicant until she learns her marriage may be invalid; then she switches from the Communion Service to the Morning Prayer Service. This is not the act of a skeptic in matters of faith. (Let me add a parentheses, if I may. Where Sayers is in this business is not a simple matter to decide--not even at the level that Brabazon presents it in his biography. Sayers was married to a divorced man whose first marriage was never annulled by the Church of England; moreover, he was the partner who was in the wrong in the divorce. Her reaction, for whatever reason, was not at the level of Mary Thoday, for she took communion during her years of living with her husband at Witham, Essex. Not all the book is autobiographical.)

The second point I want to make about the religious reading is that it explains--at a different level--the emphasis on chance I found in the detective plot. If God's providence rules this book, then it is not accident that Deacon writes an elaborate but valid cipher, that Cranton drops it in the bell-chamber, that Hilary Thorpe finds it and sends it to Lord Peter, that the rector should come in when Wimsey has it arranged in columns of eight and near-sightedly think it a chart of bell-changes. These things and others are not by chance, as in a Thomas Hardy novel, but by Providence, if one accepts Mr. Venables' views. Of course, literally the question is left open: his view is only one of those in the novel.

I promised another reference to his views, however. At the end of the novel, after he has learned of the cause of Deacon's death, the rector says, "Perhaps God speaks through those mouths of inarticulate metal. He is a righteous judge, strong and patient, and is provoked every day." Here at the end, the humor of the character is dropped in his seriousness. No longer does he use the paraphrases of Providence; he speaks directly of God. And from his point of view (at least), what I have called the Gothic approach fuses with the Christian. It is not the bells themselves which have killed Geoffrey Deacon; it is God through the instrumentality of the bells.

I realize I have not exhausted the Christian interpretation of the book. At least three critics—the two dissertation writers, and John Cawelti in a book on popular fiction—try to fuse the detective story and the providential novel. Cawelti phrases it best when he credits God as the killer of Geoffrey Deacon; he speaks of "the final twist [of the plot] by which it becomes apparent that God is the least likely person." That is clever, but in comparison to Mr. Venables' words about God in the position of a righteous judge, not in the derogatory role of killer, it seems to trivialize the conclusion.

I would suggest briefly three other Christian aspects of the novel, all concerned with the church in the book as a symbol of the Christian faith. When Mrs. Venables shows Lord Peter around the church, much is made of the history of the various parts, and how the rector has removed some ugly additions from one period or another and restored other parts. May this not be taken as a symbol of the church, not merely as a building, or of the Christian faith, through the ages, needing protection and upkeep so it can be handed on?

Second, the ringing of bell changes is not a way of playing tunes on bells but of working out patterns "in mathematical completeness and mechanical perfection." Sayers describes it, if done correctly, as an "intricate ritual faultlessly performed." So far as I am aware, Sayers was not yet under the influence of Charles Williams when she wrote this book; indeed, it was probably because of a letter he wrote upon reading it that they met. But Williams' epigram, "Hell is always inaccurate," and its converse, that Heaven is always precise, suggests why they had something in common.

Third, near the end of the book a flood in the fens causes the parishioners to take refuge in the church, which is on high ground. The parallels to Noah's flood are made, including Wimsey bringing back some laurels from a front garden, in lieu of an olive branch, when he discovers the waters have gone down an inch. May this not be taken as a symbol of the Church as a place of refuge in troubled times?

These symbols, if I am right, of the Church as eternal through the ages but always needing repair, of it as mathematical and precise in its statements, and of it as a refuge, are in addition to the themes of God's providence.

At this point I seem to have finished the topic I announced. **The Nine Tailors** is complex because it can be approached as detective fiction, a local-color novel, an autobiographical work, a Gothic novel, and a Christian statement. These are five approaches. But I said at the first that I saw five or perhaps six levels of meaning. I would like to close with that sixth possibility.

When Hilary Thorpe finds the cipher in the bell-chamber, she is described this way: "Hilary was standing in a splash of sunshine that touched the brazen mouth of Tailor Paul [one of the bells] and fell about her like Danae's shower." Thus a simile, reminding the reader of Zeus's golden love for a mortal maiden. By the end of the novel Hilary has not only inherited from her parents, who have left her mainly financial problems, but unexpectedly from an elderly aunt, who has left her wealthy. The shower from Zeus—or, more accurately in this novel, from the Christian God—has been golden indeed. Since I argue from a simile once used, perhaps I may say that this is another way in which this novel may be taken to be what Sayers called it, a "poetic romance."

A CHECKLIST OF CRITICISM REFERRED TO IN THE ESSAY

Barzun, Jacques, and Wendell Hertig Taylor. **A Book of Prefaces to "Fifty Classics of Crime Fiction, 1900-1950."** New York: Garland Publishing, 1976. (See the preface to Sayers' **Strong Poison**, p. 97.)

Brabazon, James. **Dorothy L. Sayers: The Life of a Courageous Woman.** London: Victor Gollancz, 1981.

Burleson, James Bernard, Jr. "A Study of the Novels of Dorothy L. Sayers." Ph.D. dissertation: The University of Texas at Austin, 1965. Copies are available through University Microfilms, No. 65-10,714.

Cawelti, John G. **Adventure, Mystery, and Romance: Formula Stories as Art and Popular Culture.** Chicago: The University of Chicago Press, 1976.

Durkin, Sister Mary Brian, O.P. **Dorothy L. Sayers.** Boston: Twayne Publishers (Twayne's English Authors Series, No. 281), 1980.

Hitchman, Janet. **Such a Strange Lady: An Introduction to Dorothy L. Sayers (1893-1957).** London: New English Library, 1975.

Hone, Ralph E. **Dorothy L. Sayers: A Literary Biography.** Kent, Ohio: The Kent State University Press, 1979.

Partridge, Ralph. "A Bumper Crop." **New Statesman and Nation,** 20 January 1934, p. 94.

Sayers, Dorothy L. "Gaudy Night." In **Titles to Fame,** ed. Denys Kilham Roberts. London: Thomas Nelson and Sons, 1937, pp. 73-95. Also reprinted (in a shortened form) in **The Art of the Mystery Story,** ed. Howard Haycraft. New York: Simon and Schuster, 1946, pp. 208-221.

Soloway, Sara Lee. "Dorothy Sayers: Novelist." Ph.D. dissertation: The University of Kentucky, 1971. Copies are available through University Microfilms, No. 71-25,919.

Wilson, Edmund. "Who Cares Who Killed Roger Ackroyd?: A Second Report on Detective Fiction." **The New Yorker,** 20 (20 January 1945): 59-65. Reprinted in his **Classics and Commercials: A Literary Chronicle of the Forties** (New York: Farrar, Straus, 1950) and in his **Literary Chronicle: 1920-1950** (New York: Doubleday Anchor, 1956.

Spy Series Characters in Hardback, Part XIV
Barry Van Tilburg

DOSSIER #64: Dr. Adolf Grundt (Clubfoot).
CREATED BY: Valentine Williams.
OCCUPATION: During World War I, Grundt ran the personal secret service of Kaiser Wilhelm, reporting directly to the Kaiser. Everyone was afraid of him, friend or foe. He was a very arrogant man who loved to torture people. Later, after the war, he turned to private enterprise and ran his own espionage service.
ASSOCIATES: Grundt had many people under him, too many to name.
WEAPONS: Grundt likes revolvers but also carries a cane which he can use quite effectively.
OTHER COMMENTS: Grundt's running adversaries (in three books) are the brothers Francis and Desmond Okewood. Grundt derived his nickname from his distinguishing deformity. Grundt runs afoul of British and American agents in the series.

The Man with the Clubfoot (Grossett & Dunlap, 1918).
The Return of Clubfoot (Herbert Jenkins, 1922).
Clubfoot, the Avenger (Herbert Jenkins, 1923).
The Crouching Beast (Grossett & Dunlap, 1925).
The Gold Comfit Box (Herbert Jenkins, 1932; published as **The Mystery of the Gold Box** by Collier, 1932).
The Spider's Touch (Houghton-Mifflin, 1936).
Courier to Marrakesh (Hodder & Stoughton, 1944).

DOSSIER #65: Ormiston.
CREATED BY: James Morgan Walsh.
OCCUPATION: Agent for British Intelligence.
ASSOCIATES: Rosalie Ormiston, his wife; Terry Vaun, his brother-in-law; Isabell Vaun, Terry's wife; and Sir Reginald Vallery, his boss.
WEAPONS: Pistols.
OTHER COMMENTS: Ormiston's bosses leave him to proceed on his own. They don't care how he does the job, as long as it gets done. As the series starts, Ormiston is working the Middle East, but later he is transferred back to England as he is needed there. Ormiston, Terry, and their wives are masters of disguise. Terry, however, is a show-off and often gets himself into situations that Ormiston has to extract him from.

Ormiston's wife Rosalie is just as good an agent as he is.

The Secret Service Girl (Nimmo, 1933).
The King's Messenger (Nimmo, 1933).
Spies Are Abroad (Nimmo, 1933).
Spies in Pursuit (Nimmo, 1934).
The Man from Whitehall (Collins, 1934).
Spies Never Return (Collins, 1935).
Tiger of the Night (Collins, 1935).
The Silent Man (Collins, 1935).
The Half Ace (Collins, 1936).
Spies' Vendetta (Collins, 1936).
Spies in Spain (Collins, 1937).

DOSSIER #66: Oliver Keene.
CREATED BY: James Morgan Walsh.
OCCUPATION: Agent for British Intelligence.
ASSOCIATES: Chief, his boss; Peter Chun, a fellow agent and sometimes partner.
WEAPONS: Pistols.
OTHER COMMENTS: O.K. is an older, corpulent agent, whereas Peter Chun is his younger, more agile fellow agent. Both have their own ways and means of investigation but can work well together as a team. The books usually start out with a murder.

Island of Spies (Collins, 1937).
Black Dragon (Collins, 1938).
Dial 999 (Collins, 1938).
Bullets for Breakfast (Collins, 1939).
King's Enemies (Collins, 1940).
Secret Weapons (Collins, 1940).
Spies from the Skies (Collins, 1941).
Death at His Elbow (Collins, 1941).
Danger Zone (Collins, 1942).
Island Alert (Collins, 1943).
Face Value (Collins, 1944).
Whispers in the Dark (Collins, 1945).

DOSSIER #67: Richard Graham.
CREATED BY: John Welcome.
OCCUPATION: Ex-jockey, adventurer, and British agent.
ASSOCIATES: Sir William Bellamy, his sometimes boss; Simon Herald, ex-agent and friend.
WEAPONS: Pistols and his hands.
OTHER COMMENTS: Graham is like a James Bond of the racing game. Later in the series he has to quit racing because of a series of accidents which almost kill him. He starts writing about the racing game for a newspaper. The newspaper articles and writing books become a cover for his intelligence operations.

Run for Cover (Faber & Faber, 1958).
Beware of Midnight (Faber & Faber, 1961).

Hard to Handlel (Faber & Faber, 1964).
Wanted for Killing (Faber & Faber, 1965; Holt, Rinehardt, and Winston, 1967).
Hell Is Where You Find It (Faber & Faber, 1967).
On the Stretch (Faber & Faber, 1969).
Go for Broke (Faber & Faber, 1972; Walker, 1972).

DOSSIER #68: Mark Corrigan.
CREATED BY: Mark Corrigan.
OCCUPATION: Starts the series as a private investigator who worked for U.S. Intelligence during the war. Later on, he works assignments free-lance for various agencies of the U.S. government.
ASSOCIATES: Tucker McLean, his female partner.
WEAPONS: Large-caliber pistols.
OTHER COMMENTS: Corrigan is an easy mark for a pretty face. Tucker is always trying to keep him out of woman troubles. The series is along the lines of a hardboiled-detective series.

Bullets and Brown Eyes (Werner Laurie, 1948).
Sinner Take All (Werner Laurie, 1949).
Lovely Lady (Werner Laurie, 1949).
The Wayward Blonde (Werner Laurie, 1950).
The Golden Angel (Werner Laurie, 1950).
Shanghai Jezebel (Werner Laurie, 1951).
Madame Sly (Werner Laurie, 1951).
Baby Face (Werner Laurie, 1952).
Lady of China Street (Werner Laurie, 1952).
All Brides Are Beautiful (Werner Laurie, 1953).
Sweet and Deadly (Werner Laurie, 1953).
I Like Danger (Werner Laurie, 1954).
The Naked Lady (Werner Laurie, 1954).
Madame and Eve (Werner Laurie, 1954).
Love for Sale (Angus & Robertson, 1955).
The Big Squeeze (Angus & Robertson, 1955).
Big Boys Don't Cry (Angus & Robertson, 1956).
Sydney for Sin (Angus & Robertson, 1956).
The Cruel Lady (Angus & Robertson, 1957).
Dumb as They Come (Angus & Robertson, 1957).
Honolulu Snatch (Angus & Robertson, 1958).
Menace in Siam (Angus & Robertson, 1958).
Singapore Downbeat (Angus & Robertson, 1959).
The Girl from Moscow (Angus & Robertson, 1959).
Sin in Hong Kong (Angus & Robertson, 1960).
Lady from Tokyo (Angus & Robertson, 1962.)

DOSSIER #69: Bruce Murdoch and Mary Dell.
CREATED BY: Norman Dean [John Creasey].
OCCUPATION: Agents for British Intelligence.
ASSOCIATES: Sir Robert Holt (The Pink 'Un), their boss; Percival Briggs, Murdoch's servant.

WEAPONS: Pistols.
OTHER COMMENTS: Murdoch, being a wealthy man at the start of the series, does not work for money but to help his country in its time of need. The stories take place during Hitler's reign of terror. Their arch-enemy is a German master-spy called "The Withered Man." There will never be another man nor writer quirte like John Creasey again.

Secret Errand (Hurst, 1939; McKay-Washburn, 1974).
Dangerous Journey (Hurst, 1939; McKay-Washburn, 1974).
Unknown Mission (Hurst, 1940, McKay-Washburn, 1973).
The Withered Man (Hurst, 1940; McKay-Washburn, 1974).
I Am the Withered Man (Hurst, 1941; McKay-Washburn, 1973).
Where Is the Withered Man? (Hurst, 1942; McKay-Washburn, 1972).

DOSSIER #70: Johnson Johnson.
CREATED BY: Dorothy Dunnet [in U.S.; Dorothy Halliday in U.K.].
OCCUPATION: Roving agent for British Intelligence.
ASSOCIATES: Spry, the skipper of his yacht, Dolly.
WEAPONS: Uses pistols, but prefers brains.
OTHER COMMENTS: Johnson is a near-sighted portrait painter who is also a roving agent. He travels with the yachting set and is a highly paid portrait painter. His yacht gives the British editions their titles.

The Photogenic Soprano (Houghton-Mifflin, 1968; published as Dolly and the Singing Bird by Joseph, 1968).
Murder in the Round (Houghton-Mifflin, 1970; published as Dolly and the Cookie Bird by Joseph, 1970).
Match for a Murderer (Houghton-Mifflin, 1971; published as Dolly and the Doctor Bird by Joseph, 1971).
Murder in Focus (Houghton-Mifflin, 1973; published as Dolly and the Starry Bird by Joseph, 1973).
Dolly and the Nanny Bird (Joseph, 1976; Knopf, 1982).

DOSSIER #71: Charlie Muffin.
CREATED BY: Brian Freemantle.
OCCUPATION: Ex-British Intelligence agent, now free-lance agent.
ASSOCIATES: None.
WEAPONS: Pistols and his brains.
OTHER COMMENTS: Charlie's wife was killed in the first book in mistake for him. This is what threw him on the run. Charlie is a ragged, burned-out agent. He is constantly on the run from British, American, and Russian agents alike. He is an agent no one wants to have but everyone wants to use.

Charlie M (Doubleday, 1977; published as Charlie Muffin by Cape, 1977).
Clap Hands, Here Comes Charlie (Cape, 1978).
The Inscrutible Charlie Muffin (Cape, 1979).
Charlie Muffin's Uncle Sam (Cape, 1980).
Madrigal for Charlie Muffin (Hutchinson, 1981).

DOSSIER #72: Lieutenant-Commander John Prentice.
CREATED BY: "Sea-Lion" [Geoffrey Masten Bennett].
OCCUPATION: Signal officer in the British Royal Navy.
ASSOCIATES: Peter Browning, a naval intelligence officer; Tania Maitland, a dancer and singer who is in love with and also helps Prentice and Browning; Sir Edward Trelawny, head of the British Foreign Office.
WEAPONS: Service revolvers.
OTHER COMMENTS: This is an excellent series on naval intelligence. Prentice in the first part of the series is more of a help-mate for Browning, but later on, since he has a feel for espionage adventures, he takes Browning's place. After Browning's death, John and Tania enter into two adventures of their own. Later, Prentice becomes a full Commander and marries Tania.

Phantom Fleet (Collins, 1946).
Sink Me the Ship (Collins, 1946).
Sea of Troubles (Collins, 1947).
Cargo for Crooks (Collins, 1948).
When Danger Threatens (Collins, 1949).

DOSSIER #73: Timothy Terrell.
CREATED BY: Stephen Maddock.
OCCUPATION: Agent for British Intelligence.
ASSOCIATES: Colonel Blount, his boss; Bisket, a helper.
OTHER COMMENTS: Terrell is really a non-violent type of agent. When force is the only alternative it is used. Terrell seems to look for his own adventures when none present themselves. Terrell can become a master of disguize. Most of Terrell's stories start with a murder.

A Woman of Destiny (Collins, 1933).
The White Siren (Collins, 1934).
Danger After Dark (Collins, 1934).
Conspirators in Capri (Collins, 1935).
The Eye at the Keyhole (Collins, 1935).
Gentlemen of the Night (Collins, 1936).
Conspirators Three (Collins, 1936).
Forbidden Frontiers (Collins, 1937).
Lamp Post 592 (Collins, 1937).
Doorway to Danger (Collins, 1938).
Spies Along the Severn (Collins, 1938).
Spades at Midnight (Collins, 1939).
Date with a Spy (Collins, 1941).
Drum Beat at Dusk (Collins, 1943).
Something on the Stairs (Collins, 1944).
I'll Never Like Friday Again (Collins, 1945).
Overture to Trouble (Collins, 1946).

Lady Molly of Scotland Yard

Earl F. Bargainnier

Published in 1910, **Lady Molly of Scotland Yard** consists of eleven stories, the last divided into two chapter.[1] Though only a minute fraction of Baroness Emmuska Orczy's vast amount of fiction, these stories are of historical importance in the detective genre, for their heroine is the first fictional woman detective at Scotland Yard.[2] The historical importance, however, is matched by critical disdain for Lady Molly Robertson-Kirk's efforts as a detective. A.E. Murch describes her as "one of the least convincing 'fair sleuths' of fiction, who relied more upon good luck and intuition than on any sound grasp of detective technique," and Julian Symons declares vehemently that she is "a woman detective more disastrously silly than most of her kind."[3] Such comments would seem to place Lady Molly outside the company of her creator's more admired and certainly better-known Old Man in the Corner and Sir Percy Blakeney, the elusive Scarlet Pimpernel. Nevertheless, the stories are worth at least a brief examination--whatever their faults--for presenting the first female detective at Scotland Yard, as well as a feminine "Watson," in British detective fiction.

The stories are narrated by Mary Granard, who is successively Lady Molly's maid, her assistant at the Yard, and her private secretary. If Lady Molly seems "silly," much of the blame must be directed at Orczy's characterization of Mary Granard and the narrative voice given her. The only appropriate adjectives for that voice are **chatty** and **cliche-ridden**, and the only noun is **gush**. She is continually **astonished** or **aghast**, finds situations **appalling, horrible, terrible, horrid,** and **awful,** is unembarrassed by such trite phrases as "fell purpose," "dastardly miscreant," and "mantle of impenetrable mystery," cosily throws in "as you know" again and again, and loves the adjective **dear,** as in "dear little convent." Needless to say, Granard's language detracts from the stories; gush and reason do not combine. If Orczy's intent was to characterize Granard by that language, to make her "feminine," she succeeded only in making her the stereotype that women of the eighties take pride in having come a long way from. Orczy also allows her to reflect all of the prejudice toward foreigners--which seems strange for an author born in Hungary--and the snobbery toward "the lower orders" associated with Imperialist Britain. Italians are Mafiosi, Jews are moneylenders (e.g., Abraham Rubinstein), and as for the French: "Pondicherry is a French settlement, and manners and customs there are often very peculiar."[p. 92] The lower classes, particularly servants and working women, are presented from a point of superiority--this despite Granard's own "working-class" position. Cooks go into hysterics and waitresses speak with "that vagueness which is a usual and highly irritating characteristic of their class."[p. 249] Miss Lulu Fay, an actress, is "an over-dressed, much behatted, peroxided young woman, who bore the stamp of the profession all over her pretty, painted face";[p. 209] the implications of prostitution in that the are impossible to ignore.

Though Granard can dismiss other women as vapid little fools, old maids, or "the silly, emotional, dear little thing,"[p. 110] she is, in spite of her elitism, a kind of feminist, at least where women as detectives are the issue: "We of the Female Department are dreadfully snubbed by the men, though don't tell me that women have not ten times as much intuition as the blundering and sterner sex."[p. 1] In the stories those men are represented by the Chief, who calls on Lady Molly when there is "a woman in the case," and the repeated Inspectors Pegram, Elliott, Saunders, and Danvers, whose function is essentially to wait until they can take the culprit away after Lady Molly has solved the case. When she solves one on the basis of the size of a woman's hat, she says, "Our fellows did not think of that, because they are men." Granard gushingly adds, "You see how simple it all was!"[p. 259] The functions of a Watson as narrator are to serve as a reader surrogate in accompanying the detective, as well as serving as a scapegoat, since the reader can feel superior to the Watson's less than adequate intelligence. Mary Granard fulfills these functions, but in such a way that one can only wonder why Lady Molly desires such an early twentieth-century Maribel Morgan as her aide and why Baroness Orczy decided so to characterize her.

Since Granard idolizes Lady Molly, she can only speak breathlessly of her appearance, manner, and ability as a detective. Lady Molly is always "my dear lady," as in "my dear lady's gentle voice, her persuasive eloquence, her kindly words"--Granard can also include herself in such praise: "two such charming English ladies as Lady Molly and myself."[pp. 236, 124] Granard does not supply Lady Molly's age, but she seems to be in her late twenties. Nor is there any detailed description of her appearance, though generalities abound: "my sweet, womanly, ultra-feminine, beautiful lady,"[p. 172] "wonderful charm of manner,"[p. 47] "her stern, luminous eyes."[p. 119]. Particular emphasis, again without detail, is placed upon her "matchless" figure and stylish clothes, as "charming, graceful and elegant in her beautiful directoire gown" and "her graceful figure, immaculately dressed in a perfect, tailor-made gown."[pp. 45, 90-91] Obviously, Lady Molly is so graceful and charming that she could as easily be a fashion model as a detective, yet while she is always "serene and placid," there is "nothing of the squeamish **grande dame**" about her when action is necessary.[p. 177] All in all, Mary Granard's presentation of Lady Molly offers the reader, to use her word, an **ultra-feminine** great detective, one whose involvement with crime never coarsens her innate gentility nor mars her fragile beauty. She is not just a lady in the sense of the nobility, but a lady in that term's most feminine connotations.

However, one has to assume that her aristocratic pedigree, at least on her father's side, is a principal reason. She is the daughter of the Earl of Flintshire and conveniently has "a small private fortune of her own."[p. 266] Her mother was a French actress who ran away with the Earl, leaving her first husband, but Lady Molly has inherited only her beauty, "none of her faults." By sheer coincidence, Lady Molly loves the grandson of that first husband, Captain Hubert de Mazareen. Because of the opposition of the grandfather to their relationship, he decides to change his will, but his lawyer is murdered just before his own death. Captain de Mazareen is convicted of the crime, but not before he and Lady Molly are secretly married. All of this information is related in the next-to-last chapter, "Sir Jeremiah's Will," and the last, "The End," presents Lady Molly's proving her husband's innocence after he has spent five years in prison.

That the wife of a convict in the first decade of the twentieth century, however much she believes him innocent, would or could become the leading female detective at Scotland Yard requires more than a willing suspension of disbelief; it demands utter credulousness. Yet readers are informed that "there was not a single member of the entire police force in the kingdom who would not have availed himself gladly of her help when confronted with a seemingly impenetrable mystery."[p. 154] Readers are asked to believe that the deference she receives from colleagues is the result of her having "worked her way upwards analyzing and studying, exercising her powers of intuition and of deduction, until at the present moment she is considered, by chiefs and men alike, the greatest authority among them on criminal investigation."[p. 275] She has achieved this preeminence as a detective in just five years, another proposition that staggers belief. Nevertheless, she receives "**carte blanche** from headquarters to do whatever she [thinks] right,"[p. 90] including such doubtful acts as having a male assistant burglarize a suspect's baggage in "The Fordwych Castle Mystery" and then accepting a gift of five thousand pounds for solving that case.

Lady Molly is fond of using disguise or impersonation (six of the eleven cases) and of laying various traps to prove guilt (five of the eleven), but, without question, her major "method" of detection is intuition. Mary Granard takes great pride in this quality of her dear lady and repeatedly praises it. From more than twenty such statements of Lady Molly's quick and keen intuition, three are more than enough examples: "a case which more than any other required feminine tact, intuition, and all those qualities of which my dear lady possessed more than her usual share"[p. 73]; "No doubt [the Chief] began to feel that here, too, was a case where feminine tact and my lady's own marvelous intuition might prove more useful than the more approved methods of the sterner sex"[p. 102]; "As usual, here scheme was bold and daring; she trusted her own intuition and acted accordingly"[p. 229]. Most women today would object to such emphasis on feminine intuition, so-called, particularly female scholars of detective fiction, who have shown that this view of women's reasoning powers is fallacious. In attempting more than seventy years ago to make an official woman detective acceptable to both male and female readers, Baroness Orczy chose to minimize those qualities which men might find threatening and most women of that time improper. Instead, she created a paragon of feminity, a devoted wife, and a vision of elegance and beauty, who has the intuitive ability to "guess" likely criminals and their methods.

Lady Molly's cases are pure puzzles of the type so popular at the time of their writing. She solves seven murders, three thefts, and a single case of blackmail. As stated earlier, impersonation plays a large part in Lady Molly's work. Whether she is pretending to be the Grand Duchess of Starkburg-Nauheim in "A Day's Folly" or a charwoman in "The Bag of Sand," she intuitively divines the culprit and proves her hypothesis by posing as someone else to entrap that culprit into giving himself or herself away or into confessing. (Some of the villains also use impersonation, including an example of transvestism in "The Man in the Inverness Cape.") With Sir Percy Blakeney, the Scarlet Pimpernel, as her prime instance, one can only assume that some form of impersonation or disguise is Orczy's favorite plot device. The repetition of the intuition-impersonation-entrapment formula does not make the stories as predictable as might be expected, for the ingenuity of the plot puzzles hides the basic formulaic structure, as a comparison of "A Day of Folly" and "The Man in the Inverness Cape," both having that same structure, clearly shows. Nor do the similar settings make the stories seem overly repetitious. Only two of the cases do not involve the wealthy or aristocratic: "The Irish-Tweed Coat," which concerns the Mafia, and "The Man in the Inverness Cape," which is about a professional thief. The others are filled with such names as Lady Irene Culloden, Lady d'Alboukirk, H.S.H. the Countess of Hohengebirg, Lord Edbrooke, Lord Ullesthorpe, and Monsieur le Marquis de Terhoven. That short list, from many, includes not just those involved, but also victims and villains; the variety of roles is another means of avoiding the predictable. Such a large number of high-ranking personages gives the impression that crime is rife amongst the upper classes, greed being the principal motive over and over. What may seem unusual at first glance is the number of women villains: four women are murderers, one a thief, one a blackmailer, and another—with her son—attempts to steal an inheritance. Apparently, Orczy wished to "even the competition": to balance her female detective with female criminals (again, five of the seven are upper class). The most interesting fact about the women whom Lady Molly confronts is that, with the possible exception of the one in "The Fordwych Castle Mystery," none are **femmes fatales**, the type of woman criminal most frequent in early twentieth-century British detective fiction, as Irene Adler or L.T. Meade and Robert Eustace's Madame Sara. The fascination is given to the heroine; her criminous rivals cannot compare.

The stories have a certain period charm (I regret having to use one of Granard's favorite words), with matinees of **Trilby**, cosy little houses in Maida Vale, elegant seaside resorts, masses of servants at country houses and castles, handsome young officers, and pretty women in distress. They are of their time and evoke it well, at least of the upper levels of its society. though present-day readers, especially feminists, may find that society as presented an element to be condemned, it is not an untruthful presentation, just a romantic one. Baroness Orczy attempted to portray a woman detective of Scotland Yard at a time when policewomen of any type were still a rarity, and, therefore, she had few models. As the image of a policewoman was—and to some still is—that of a coarse, "unfeminine" woman, she went to the other extreme: making Lady Molly Robertson-Kirk the epitome of genteel femininity, particularly by Mary Granard's adoration of her. The puzzles of her cases are ingenious, if repetitive, but her detection is light. It is as if once the Baroness had invented her female "great detective," she did not know how to justify the greatness in a way that would be acceptable to her readers. Lady Molly was a noble (pardon the pun) experiment, but ultimately a failure as a detective who detects.

NOTES

[1]The edition used is the 1976 Arno Press reprint of the Popular Edition published by Cassell and Company, Ltd., in 1926. All quotations are cited in the text. A paperback reprint was published by

International Polygonics, Ltd., of New York in 1981.

²I am aware that some purists might argue that Mrs. Paschal of **The Revelations of a Lady Detective** (1861) should receive this honor, but her work with the "Metropolitan Police's Detective Branch" at Whitehall came before "Scotland Yard" developed as the universal epithet for the Metropolitan Police.

³**The Development of the Detective Novel** (New York: Greenwood Press, 1958), p. 212; **Mortal Consequences** (New York: Harper & Row, 1972), p. 82. E.F. Bleiler says of the stories, "they are mildly feminist in attitude, but overwritten and sentimental" (**Twentieth Century Crime and Mystery Writers**, edited by John M. Reilly [New York: St. Martin's, 1980], p. 1142. In **The Lady Investigates: Women Detectives and Spies in Fiction** (London: Gollancz, 1981), Patricia Craig and Mary Cadogan say that "everything that worked with Sir Percy seems to have misfired with Lady Molly."[p. 29]

IT'S ABOUT CRIME
by Marvin Lachman

NOTES ON RECENT READING

Many current writers try to **shock** their readers, perhaps believing that by now people are so jaded that it is the only way to get their attention. In the past, authors like Erle Stanley Gardner built their careers on **surprise**, and there is a world of difference. **Shock** (it rhymes with "schlock") is relatively easy. All an author has to do is to think of something outrageous or unlikely. How much more difficult is it to build a career on the **surprise** that comes from careful plotting and the juggling of many clues and alibis. Yet Gardner did this, and he was an outstanding storyteller for almost fifty years. That is why I am so glad to see Ballantine continue to reprint the Perry Mason canon, with the cases of **The Lonely Heiress** (1948) and **The Dubious Bridegroom** (1949) being the latest releases.

I don't believe in telling much about plots in my reviews, and it's even less necessary than usual with a Perry Mason book. I'll admit that one of his plots was seldom especially different from the next (or the last). They certainly weren't very exotic. Ah, but the pleasure of seeing a master ring countless variations and the narrative drive are what makes Gardner worthwhile. It all culminates in beautifully handled courtroom scenes, and you'll even learn a bit of law. **Dubious Bridegroom** is one of his better books, and **Heiress** is not too far behind.

For a new generation which has never read Gardner (he has been dead more than thirteen years), I recommend trying one of the books. You may become pleasantly hooked. Don't be put off if you've seen the ridiculous courtroom confessions during some of the endless repeats of the Mason TV shows. They don't occur in the books. Gardner had too much respect for his readers' intelligence.

Rex Stout was never as good a plotter or storyteller as his contemporary, Gardner. He succeeded because of the unforgettable eccentricity of his main character and the wonderful Wolfe-Archie relationship he developed. That is why non-Wolfe books like **The Sound of Murder**, while generally interesting and readable, are not in a class with the Wolfe series. Bantam has recently reprinted **The Sound of Murder** (1941), and they've added an extra element of mystery. On the cover they give the book's original title, but they get it wrong! They called it **Alphabet Jackson**. Of course, the original title was **Alphabet Hicks**, after the series detective in this book and at least one other Stout short story, "By His Own Hand," reprinted in **EQMM** (May 1964) as "Curtain Line."

But, then, one should never judge a Bantam book by its cover.

Their fourteenth reprint of the Ross Macdonald book **The Chill** (1964) has an ugly, inappropriate cover, but within is one of the best private eye novels ever written.

A year after this book, Macdonald was "discovered" by the intelligensia. (Boucher had been touting him for fifteen years.) It may be coincidence, but then the Lew Archer series dropped in quality and became repetitive. At the time of **The Chill**, however, Ross Macdonald was still at his peak.

At the time of another Bantam Ross Macdonald reprint, **The Three Roads** (1948), Archer was still a gleam in his creator's mind. The book was originally published under Macdonald's real name, Kenneth Millar. The plot is very 1940-ish, about the Navy officer with psychological problems who finds his wife murdered and must find the killer while escaping suspicion himself. If not quite the equal of **The Chill**, **The Three Roads** is still a marvelous book, with its incisive characterization, sharp dialogue, and perceptive view of Southern California. The cover: another mistake; it's a symbolic Pop-Art scene of cigarettes and an ash tray. That's all.

Does anyone else have trouble selecting which book should be read from among their vast piles and shelves of unread mysteries? I normally do, but the choice was fairly easy as to what I should bring on a recent long weekend at my in-laws in Western Pennsylvania. Consider the following:

1. They live near Pittsburgh.
2. I had just seen a performance by the New Jersey Symphony of Prokofiev's **Alexander Nevsky**.
3. I had just received a review copy from Avon of Dimitri Gat's **Nevsky's Demon** (1983), and I hadn't as yet read the first in what was becoming a series.

So, beloved reader, what book did I take along? Right, I took Gat's **Nevsky's Return**, published by Avon in 1982 as a paperback original, the first in a series about Yuri Nevsky, a Pittsburgh detective.

A refreshing trend in recent years has been taking private eyes from the much used (and abused) California scene. The Albert Sampson Indianapolis and Harry Stoner Cincinnati series come to mind. Now we have Pittsburgh, and Gat captures many of its characteristics, e.g., its hills, rivers, air quality, love affair with football, etc. **Nevsky's Return** is about an enclave called "Russian Slope" of which my in-laws have never heard. Does it exist, Walter Albert? Still, Gat brings it alive, whether fictional or not, and he does a nice job of blending Russian-American culture into a mystery plot.

I hope the character, Yuri Nevsky, can sustain a series. Except for his unusual ethnic background, he is like many of his detective forefathers. He has the guilt trips, broken marriage, tendency to get slugged, etc. Actually, he doesn't consider himself a private eye, calling himself "The World's First Reluctant Investigator" in a nice bit of self-deprecating humor. He thinks of himself, euphemistically, as being in the information—not the investigation—business.

I like the idea of a private eye writer named "Gat." I also liked **Nevsky's Return** well enough to put its sequel in a higher spot on my to-be-read pile.

In 1982, once again, most of my short-story reading was in EQMM. If my lack of variety is the bad news, the good news is that EQMM continues to offer a great deal that is worthwhile. If anything, during its forty-second year EQMM was better than at any time since its golden age, 1946-1957. The following dozen, in order of quality, were the best stories of the year in EQMM, but I probably could have come up with another dozen almost as good:

1. Julian Symons, "The Flaw"
2. Jack Ritchie, "A Case of Identity"
3. Ruth Rendell, "The Man Who Frightened Women"
4. F.B. Roome, "Dead Man's Walk"
5. Clark Howard, "Old Soldiers"
6. Clark Howard, "All the Heroes Are Dead"
7. Simon Brett, "Escape Route"
8. Donald Westlake, "Re Porter"
9. Robert Twohy, "The Bathtub Murders"
10. Edward D. Hoch, "The Problem of the Gypsy Camp"
11. Edward D. Hoch, "The Flying Fiend"
12. James Powell, "Pocketful of Noses"

As I've warned in the past, one misses an issue of EQMM at one's own risk, since one never knows what gem one will find. Take this year's best, the Symons story, which, in its own way, was flawless.

NOTES ON RECENT VIEWING

The PBS series **Mystery** did a good job of televising Antonia Fraser's **Quite as a Nun**, due mainly to a fine performance by Maria Aitkin as Jemima Shore. She not only delivered her lines well, she also appeared to be really listening to her fellow actors when they spoke. So many actors on TV are clearly only waiting to deliver their own next line.

Television really emphasized the good and bad points in Fraser's first mystery. On the positive side was atmosphere and an unusual background, an English Catholic school. On the negative side was the book's ending, which seemed even weaker on the screen. It was difficult to tell the nuns apart because their habits covered so much of their faces and figures. The series was remarkably close to the book, only changing Shore to a smoker from a non-smoker for some unfathomable reason.

Publicity about Lady Fraser has stressed her own "liberated" qualities. Yet, in both book and television Jemima wanders about at night, screams and faints when frightened, and gets hit on the head. Had I but known Lady Antonia was going to borrow from Mary Roberts Rinehart ....

One never knows when something mystery-related will show up on video. An old Universal Deanna Durbin musical, **Something in the Wind** (1947), surprisingly included a very young Donald O'Connor doing a funny musical number called "I Love a Mystery." It was a spoof of mysteries in general, rather than the old radio program of the same name. Done very energetically in a fashion similar to O'Connor's unforgettable "Make 'Em Laugh" in **Singin' in the Rain** (1952), it ends with him wearing a Holmesian deerstalker. The number has nothing to do with the rest of the plot of this insipid little film, but it brightens it immeasurably.

I only caught three of the five **Philip Marlowe, Private Eye** episodes in the series on HBO, but they were good enough to make me anticipate the inevitable re-runs on that cable network. They moved quickly and caught a lot of the flavor of Los Angeles in the past by their location shots (interiors were actually filmed in London). I could have done without the James Bond-type opening credits. Powers Boothe as Marlowe looked a bit bored, but I liked Kathryn Leigh Scott as his friend, Annie Riordan, in "The Pencil" and was especially glad that all five episodes were based on original Chandler stories.

DEATH OF A MYSTERY WRITER

1. **Zelda Popkin** at age 84 in Silver Spring, Maryland, May 25, 1983. Born in New York in 1895, she started out, at age 17, as a reporter on the Wilkes-Barre **Times Leader.** She entered the Columbia School of Journalism at age 19.

Married to Louis Popkin, she worked with her husband in the public relations business in New York until his death in 1943. At the same time she wrote fiction and articles, including a series of five mysteries, beginning with **Death Wears a Gardenia** (1938), about a department store detective, Mary Carner. She also wrote one excellent mystery short story, "Junie No-Name," which was a Third Prize winner in EQMM's contest for 1953 and appeared in February 1954. Her later fiction generally dealt with Israel and Jewish life, though one novel, **Death of Innocence** (1971), was about a crime and had a courtroom setting. It was filmed by CBS as a television movie.

2. **Robert Carson** at age 73 in Los Angeles. Best known for his Academy Award-winning script for the original 1937 version of **A Star Is Born,** Carson made two trips into the field of the mystery novel. The last, **The Golden Age Caper** (1970), is one of the books in the small sub-genre about geriatric crime. He wrote many screen plays and magazine stories, including "Aloha Means Goodbye," about a Japanese attack on Pearl Harbor. It appeared in the **Saturday Evening Post** in June 1941, six months **before** their actual bombing, and formed the basis of a Humphrey Bogart film, **Across the Pacific** (1942).

3. **Michael Blankfort** at age 74 in Los Angeles on July 13, 1982. In addition to many novels and screen plays (including **Broken Arrow** and **Tribute to a Bad Man,** Blankfort wrote at least one mystery, **The Widow-Makers** (1946), a book highly praised by Anthony Boucher.

4. **Jack Ritchie,** whose real name was John Reitci, at age 61 in Milwaukee on April 23, 1983. A prolific short-story writer (he wrote more than five hundred), he won an Edgar in 1982 for "The Absence of Emily," which appeared the previous year in EQMM.

REEL MURDERS

MOVIE REVIEWS by Walter Albert

Stanley Kubrick has been one of the most admired and respected film directors for at least twenty years, with a record that few contemporary filmmakers can match. His first major critical breakthrough was the striking anti-war film, **The Paths of Glory** (1957), which can be honorably compared to Lewis Milestone's **All Quiet on the Western Front** (1931) and Jean Renoir's **Grande Illusion** (1937), but his acceptance by both critics and audiences probably dates from 1963 and his savagely funny **Dr. Strangelove, or How I Learned to Stop Worrying and Love the Bomb**. This success was confirmed with one of the most innovative and influential films of the period, **2001: A Space Odyssey** (1968), a success that has not been matched for the critics or the public by any of the three films he has directed since then: **A Clockwork Orange** (1971), **Barry Lyndon** (1975), or **The Shining** (1980). Indeed, the massive failure of **Barry Lyndon** to find an audience in this country and the critical disapproval that greeted his filming of Stephen King's book **The Shining** have appeared to provoke a reassessment of his work by many critics that can probably be best summed up by the observation that there may be less in his films than meets the eye. **Barry Lyndon** was generally thought to be a beautiful but vapid film with an eccentric casting of Ryan O'Neal as the ambitious, doomed Barry, a performance that, according to a similar critical opinion, was perhaps equalled in its inappropriateness by Jack Nicholson in **The Shining**.

I don't intend to devote this column to a defense of Kubrick's recent films--although I will say that I think **Barry Lyndon** is one of the most underrated films of the past decade--but rather to turn to his third feature-length film, **The Killing** (1956). **The Killing** is a black-and-white film (does anyone remember that black-and-white used to be the preferred medium for films?) based on Lionel White's caper novel, **Clean Break**, with a script by Kubrick and additional dialogue by writer Jim Thompson.

After a series of short documentaries growing out of his work as a photographer for **Look** magazine, Kubrick filmed a claustrophobic war drama (**Fear and Desire**, (1953), of which there seem to be no prints for public viewing, and **Killer's Kiss** (1955), a melodrama of a "girl ... kidnapped by the sadistic owner of a dance hall and rescued ... by a gallant young boxer." However, **The Killing** seems to be the earliest film that Kubrick is willing to acknowledge as his own, and, coming at the end of the great period of **films noir** which preceded Hollywood's capitulation to the seductions of color, it is one of the best of the post-war "B" films and, in its bold dislocation of chronology, a film that, at moments, has some of the freshness and excitement of the

New Wave French films of the late fifties and early sixties. The French renaissance was in large part due to the influence of the post-war American "B" films that were a revelation to the directors, and **The Killing** is clearly, in its conventions and style, related to the work of other American directors of the period.

The Killing is the story of a meticulously planned impossible robbery: of the office of a race-track whose security is thought to be unassailable. While **The Killing** is a well-crafted caper film that might appear to be limited in conception and execution (a usual criticism of genre films), the boldness of the planning and accomplishing of the robbery are not unlike the risks that Kubrick has taken in film after film: the slave whose vagabond army challenges the legions of Rome (**Spartacus**); the filming of Nabokov's perverse and witty **Lolita**, whose subject was hardly the kind to be approved by the Legion of Decency or the United Mothers of America; the unsettling blend of beauty and violence in **A Clockwork Orange** and **The Shining**; the anarchistic comedy of **Dr. Strangelove** and the Olympian, epic canvas of **Barry Lyndon**; and, of course, the imaginative rehabilitation of the science-fiction film in **2001**. All of these films, so stylistically diverse and so difficult for an auteur-oriented criticism to assimilate, are so many challenges to the established and the conventional. They may be thought to be self-fulfilling fantasies, but there is a common thread running through these films from the earliest to the most recent in the impossible attempted and failed. But with all of his attraction to the difficult and the resistant, Kubrick's intelligence is not seduced by these visions. There is a lucidity in his recognition of the traps the great projects pose that is reflected in an ironic detachment that seems to enclose his films, even at their most outrageous and troubling, in a harmoniously balanced form. His comedy sense works against comic release; his sense of the horrific almost seems to be devoid of terror and fear.

The conspirators are led by Sterling Hayden as Johnny Clay, a petty crook whose name is an all to accurate gauge of his prospects. His unimposing gang—Jay C. Flippen, Joe Sawyer, Ted de Corsia, Elisha Cook, Jr.—is perfectly cast from among the character actors who worked in films where their perfect control of an essential character could do much to salvage a film starring Hollywood's latest vapidly empty romantic team. There is not a single flaw in the casting—although the film itself is not without weaknesses—and the most surprising pairing of Elisha Cook, Jr., and Marie Windsor. Cook is a race-track employee whose dream of making it seem to have gone down the same chute as his marriage. Windsor is a posing, mocking bitch who deceives her husband with a small-time hood (Vince Edwards) and betrays the details of the plan her deluded husband reveals to her in an ill-considered moment. Windsor is herself deceived by Edwards, a betrayal she is as aware of, at times, as Cook is of her true feelings for him. But the husband and wife are also wedded to their dreams and the flaw in the concept of the robbery is not in the plan but in human nature and, more distressingly, a bored and vengeful deity, Chance, that a dozen times in the film works against the project and its participants.

Lovers of a tight narrative in which there are no embarrassing moments of slack will not be happy with **The Killing**, where Kubrick is not afraid to linger over a sentimental scene (involving Flippen's sick wife) that is ironically countered by a Cook-Windsor confrontation; to introduce an overly friendly parking-lot attendant to interfere with one of the carefully timed "events," or a traffic jam to delay Hayden's return with the money; and, finally, to use a fat lady and a small, pampered dog to expose Hayden in the final moments of the film when he might be close to escaping with the money. These gimmicks don't always work: the parking-lot attendant is played by black actor James Edwards, whose speedy warming-up to a white mobster (they are both cripples) is unconvincing in the climate of the fifties; and the woman and dog are too obviously planted and the reversal too clearly telegraphed to the audience. But it might also be argued that these less-than-convincing details are a perfect demonstration of Kubrick's belief in an almost diabolically conscious fate that takes its pleasure in blatantly countering the human actors' futile attempts to work out their own destiny. And the most striking shot in the film looks like a still photograph of the conspirators lying dead in a confused jumble, sprawled near the hoods who came to take the money from them.

At the center of the film is the performance of Sterling Hayden, an earnest, unpretentious master of the game who can bring off the robbery but not carry off the spoils. Hayden does make a killing, but there is also the brutal slaughter, and it is difficult not to see the climax of the film in the room where the bloodied, wounded Elisha Cook, along with the audience, stares in horror at the tangled bodies, rather than in the impersonal, busy air terminal where Hayden's final moves are checkmated. The final shot is brilliant: as Hayden turns to the doors leading to the terminal, he sees two security men approaching. They frame the words THE END superimposed on the shot and they are the final punctuation for the film as surely as they punctuate Hayden's collapse. In these final minutes we first seem him from the rear, his body sagging, almost without life, and when he turns to the camera and his captors he turns accepting the defeat that has crushed him.

There is one technique in particular that sets this film apart from other caper films I have seen. Our pleasure in this kind of film is usually in the planning of the caper and in our close attendance upon its execution and the aftermath. We expect to follow the timed and coordinated execution as if we were ourselves participants. Kubrick, in an unsettling and exciting denial of those expectations, films the robbery from different points of view, backing up in time to show the different strategies which lead to the robbery. Kubrick has shrugged off any credit for this technique, saying that it was this narrative shifting that had interested him in White's novel. The technique may be adapted, but that does not lessen its cinematic effectiveness.

The Killing is a film with so many fine things that only a few can be noted: the performance by Kola Kwariani as Maurice, a bald, bullet-headed chess player who stages a row to distract the police from Hayden's moves; Coleen Gray's small but important role as Hayden's girl friend who is only on screen in the beginning and at the end but who is a perfect frame as her fears, expressed in her first scene, are realized at the conclusion; the marvelous use of interiors, in particular Hayden's apartment which seems to be a series of interconnecting rooms that in spite of their perfect articulation are only vaguely defined and have something of the inevitability of a labyrinth; the bar at the racetrack that opens out toward the track like a stage on which some of the most important scenes of the film are played; and the frantic speed of the horses with their anonymous riders, always viewed from a distance, their movements described by an announcer with some of that detachment that seems so characteristic of Kubrick.

Whatever faults **The Killers** may have, it is, after thirty years, and a generation's experiences with Kubrick's films, an exciting and rich work. **The Killers**, drawing from the past and revelatory of
[Continued on page 50]

VERDICTS Book Reviews

Barbara Paul. **The Fourth Wall.** Doubleday, 1979.

Though some of her novels mix mystery and suspense with science fiction, Barbara Paul's novel **The Fourth Wall** is straight crime fiction, and it's a terrific novel. Abby James is an omnivorous reader, a book collector, a staunch friend, and a playwright whose most recent work is running on Broadway quite successfully until devastating harassment and eventually murder bedevil cast and crew. To defend her production and to protect her life, Abby pursues the killer and finds even greater danger than she anticipated.

Adept at her craft, sophisticated, mature, and self-possessed, Abby perceives herself as a fairly adroit student of human nature. She learns a good deal, however, about the effects of love, fear, possessiveness, greed, and ambition upon the human animal. While she gains awareness, she also sustains considerable loss—acquaintances die; friends are maimed; colleagues disappear; and Abby risks the most insidious decay of her own ethics and character. All this is strong stuff, and Paul takes it seriously without sacrificing tension, pace, or suspense. If, in Paul's judgment, evil is potentially contagious, as the theme of this book suggests, it is also her judgment that them should be firmly embedded in action.

Amid the blood and terror, Paul also depicts a committed writer at work, the pressures demanding that life go on even in the face of crippling pressures, and vivid details of life backstage. All these embellish and extend the plot. It's all **very** satisfactory. (Jane S. Bakerman)

Liza Cody. **Dupe.** Warner, 1983, $2.50.

Originally published in 1981, Liza Cody's **Dupe** won the John Creasey Award as the best British first mystery novel of the year. Every fan, critic, writer, reviewer, and editor has her own choice of "best," of course, but this book really is worthy. If Cody has a series in mind, there's potential here, and fans are in for a treat.

Anna Lee is a private investigator for a London firm whose employees range from admirable through irksome to downright unlikable, a nice, realistic touch probably applicable to anyone's workplace. Anna's efforts to investigate the recent life and death of Deidre, a young, film-struck dropout who has been somewhat estranged from her family, are also portrayed realistically. London weather is not romanticized for either better or worse, but it is detailed in almost every scene, lending a sense of immediacy to the plot. As Anna penetrates some distant fringes of the English film scene, she meets a number of memorable, carefully drawn characters and displays her professional skills. Those skills are considerable but not overwhelming. She's strong, capable, intelligent, determined, but not given to amazing leaps of the imagination or stupefyingly brilliant deductions. In short, like so many satisfying fictional characters, she's "one of us," but with a job more intriguing than those most of us hold.

Like many of the female private eyes who are appearing in growing numbers in recent fiction, Anna is subjected to the same lumps--physical, emotional, professional--as have become standard for her male counterparts. Furthermore, Anna can and does bleed; she does think about what she should wear; she does favors for her neighbors (usually small repairs around the place); she frets over her car--in short, she is three dimensional, lives a fairly completely drawn life, and gives every evidence of being worth knowing better. Competent plotting, sound characterization, and considerable suspense are the defining elements of **Dupe**; Cody is off to a good start. (Jane S. Bakerman)

Jonathan Valin. **Final Notice**. Avon, 1982.

If it's fun to speculate with George Grella that Lew Archer is really the illegitimate son of Sam Spade and Iva Archer, then it's equally intriguing to wonder if Spenser doesn't have a cousin who is alive and well and living in Cincinnati. His name is Harry Stoner, and he's a real man, even though he probably eats quiche. Don't mistake me; Stoner is not a copy of Spenser; he's too vivid, too fully rounded in his own personality for that. But Stoner and Spenser are lucky enough to have been created by Jonathan Valin and Robert B. Parker, writers with the wit, energy, and skill to contribute to a well-established genre not only by following its rich traditions but also by reflecting their own times.

In **The Lime Pit**, also recently available from Avon Books, Stoner solves a murder by following a slightly cold trail and loses a lover. In **Final Notice**, he solves an old murder by following a terrifyingly rewarming trail and gains a lover. Other deaths occur: Stoner withstands a terrible beating as well as a certain amount of emotional buffeting, but he preserves his professional pride and pulls his life together with grace exercised under pressure. Along the way, he does a lot of speculating about the attraction and the demands of his job, about why he **needs** to be a private investigator:

> It seemed to me, then, that vocations were a kind of camouflage that most people evolved throughout a lifetime of little hurts and triumphs, spun out of themselves the way a spider spins its web. And that for me, with my ingrown passion for finding things out, the job was no more or less than my way of tackling the mystery of knowing anyone at all. That, in spite of the cynical cracks, mine was essentially a lively business and, deep down, a moral art. [p.41]

In **Final Notice**, Stoner's business begins as an assignment to track down the defacer of expensive art books belonging to a branch of the Hamilton County library system. Leon Ringold, head of the branch, hires Stoner personally, in part to strike back against the "official" investigator, Kate Davis, of whom he disapproves and in whom he has little confidence. From the outset, Stoner resists this kind of chauvinism, even when Davis proves to be prickly, sometimes foolhardy, and usually stubborn; perhaps Harry Stoner is successful in accepting Kate Davis on almost equal terms because she shares many of his personal characteristics. Almost immediately, Stoner and his police sources discover a probable connection between the defacer and the Ripper, who, seven years before, committed a particularly brutal murder in the neighborhood, and the race is on to keep the killer from striking again. Stoner and his police buddies are not wholly successful, but the killer is subdued and order is restored--though both Stoner and Davis pay a price, in true mean-streets tradition.

Like Spade, Archer, and Spenser, Harry Stoner is a good detective who counts but accepts the cost of his calling and of his code; in his hands, as in theirs, his trade is "a moral art." (Jane S. Bakerman)

George Baxt. **The Affair at Royalties.** MacMillan, 1971.

First, a true confession: I can abide the Agatha Christie type of British village "polite" mystery only when it is written by Christie herself or when the approach is parodic-comedic. This book is of the latter type.

The cover blurb calls it "a novel of Suspense and Lost Memory," and the book delivers little of the first (opting instead for humor) and handles the other as merely an exercise of manipulation. Yet. Yet it is a fine book, and I recommend it highly. The heroine (and amnesiac) is an American writer specializing in crime and living in England (Royalties' is the name of her cottage), a parallel to Baxt. But her specialty is the re-examination of real-life crimes, especially murder. She is, thus, well-equipped for her amateur-detective central role in this story. She is also, at least briefly, a leading suspect herself.

She was found in her own blood-spattered kitchen holding a bloody knife, several days before the story actually begins. For a long time it is uncertain whether there even was a murder, but the reader understands there was (and who the victim was, and even most likely who did the killing) well before it is clear to any of the investigators. Besides the heroine, these include the obligatory Scotland Yard detective, the heroine's estranged husband (who found her in the incriminating circumstances), a nurse who is actually a policewoman in drag, and various policemen who report to the Yard man.

The suspects are the quirky lot that Baxt delights in and delights his readers with. A fishing-boat captain who is retired from a seagoing career and who hates the sea and had been having an affair with the authoress. A sculptor in the throes of his magnum opus, who may have been having an affair with her and maybe with the eventually identified victim. The sculptor's twin sister, who is also his life-long incestuous lover and has more eccentricities than even an artist would have in an ordinary mystery of this sort. A randy woman painter who specializes in flowers for greeting-card manufactures and who had been living with her "niece" in a sort of armed truce. And so on and so on.

Various of this parade of cockeyed creatures (to borrow from the title of another of Baxt's novels) serve briefly as point-of-view characters, but most of the story centers around the efforts of the heroine to figure out what set off her amnesia. The most humorous scenes are those in which the woman painter tries repeated and unsuccessful seductions of various male characters, and the violent arguments between the twins.

What Baxt does best is to get inside the minds of grotesques. He does quite a bit of it here and yet manages a passable mystery puzzle at the same time. If your British mysteries don't have to be serious (and stultifyingly dull), you should enjoy reading **The Affair at Royalties.** (Jeff Banks)

Ron Goulart, Ed. **The Great British Detectives.** New American Library, 1982, $3.95.

Heavily relying on the classical form, this volume of fifteen stories shows what gave the British their reputation for excellence at crime. Starting, of course, with Sherlock Holmes, we have appearances by such acknowledged greats as Dr. Thorndyke, Martin Hewitt, Father Brown, Mr. Fortune, Hercule Poirot, Lord Peter Wimsey, Mr. Campion, and Dr. Gideon Fell. Bringing it up to date (and the only entry written after 1940) is Ruth Rendell's Inspector Wexford in a very modern story of the old murder-or-suicide plot. These stories are all classics, worthy of reading, and probably already reread several times.

What makes the collection valuable is the addition of several stories otherwise difficult to locate, such as "Drawn Daggers" by C.L. Pirkis, featuring Loveday Brooke, and one of the Colonel Clay stories from **An African Millionaire** by Grant Allen. One of the greatest oddities is William Murray Grayham's story, "The Rajah's Bodyguard," a melodramatic, improbable Sexton Blake adventure from 1906. The story itself isn't exceptional, but it is nice for Americans to get a taste of this legendary hero. Another rarity is "The Clue of the Silver Spoons," a Eugene Valmont story by Robert Barr, only once previously printed in the U.S. Again, it is time this oft-mentioned detective was made available to the public.

An appendix lists the novels and short-story collections of each of these sleuths (with the exception of Sexton Blake), lists now available elsewhere. While there are only a few new treats here, the balance of the stories are ones that can be reread endlessly. (Fred Dueren)

Claudia Schmolders and Christian Strich, Eds. **Uber Simenon** [On Simenon] (Diogenes Taschenbuch 154). Zurich: Diogenes Verlag AG, 1978, 239 pp.

One of the series of German-language critical essay collections published by Diogenes on individual writers, several of whom are mystery writers, **Uber Simenon** contains a wealth of critical material on the author of the Maigret novels. All the material not originally written in German has been translated into German. In addition to the text of a talk Simenon gave in New York City in 1945, and an interview with French mystery critic Francis Lacassin, this volume contains extended quotes about Simenon from such prominent figures as Andre Gide, Jean Cocteau, Henry Miller, C.P. Snow, C. Day Lewis, Patricia Highsmith, and Federico Fellini.

Of the sixteen critical essays, only seven treat significantly of Simenon's detective stories. The others deal with him primarily as a novelist and compare him to Balzac, Chekhov, and Dostoyevsky. The seven criminous essays are: Francois Body, "Das Wunder Simenon"; Luke Parsons, "Simenon and Chandler"; Jean Amery, "Das fleissige Leben des Georges Simenon"; Hans Altenheim, "Ein Traum von Maigret"; Julian Symons, "Simenon und sein Maigret" (excerpt from Symons' **Bloody Murder**); Pierre Boileau, "Etwas hat sich geandert im Kriminalroman"; and Georg Hensel, "Simenon und sein Kommissar Maigret."

There is a bibliography of primary and secondary sources which is divided into nine parts. It includes the criminous and noncriminous novels, nonfictional writings and interviews, a filmography, a list of stage plays, a list of languages into which Simenon has been translated (forty-three!), and a multi-language bibliography of secondary sources articles and monographs.

Although the seven criminous essays are more descriptive than critical, two of them are especially interesting. Amery relates interesting facts and anecdotes, such as the time when Simenon was too busy to take a call from Alfred Hitchcock, and Altenheim's dreamy, surrealistic critical style is something very rarely seen in English-language mystery criticism. Apart from Amery's mis-dating by one year (too early) the date of Simenon's first Maigret novel, there were no glaring errors that I could detect. The character of Simenon as a true phenomenon in detective fiction as well as in world literature clearly emerges from this volume. (Greg Goode)

Eileen Dewhurst. **Curtain Fall**. Doubleday/Crime Club, 1982 [originally published in 1977], 186 pp., $10.95.

Theatrical murder mysteries have always possessed something a bit out of the ordinary, or so it's seemed to me. I don't think I'm alone, either--witness the continued popularity of many of Ngaio Marsh's stories built about nefarious backstage doings, just for example.

Although I'd never really thought about it before, part of the reason for all this might be that hinted at by one of the leading characters in **Curtain Fall**: actors (like murderers) are people whose lives are pretending to be what they are not.

It should be noted, however, that when this book begins there is no indication that it has anything to do with the stage or the theatre at all. Joanna Stuart is having a severe case of the middle-age blahs, and in a dreamlike trance she suddenly takes off for a vacation by the sea, almost as though she were travelling into another dimension. Quite naturally (or so it almost seems), murder intrudes.

There is no real detection involved, at least so far as the reader is concerned. Everything is wrapped up with a simple reconstruction of the crime. Nevertheless, thanks to the host of theatrical folk that Joanna discovers in her haven of refuge, this is an unusually engrossing piece of work.

And, while it may not be wholly relevant to the mystery itself, there is a final revelation that comes as much of a pleasurable surprise as the opening is both haunting and lyrical. Rather obscurely--permit my own small fancies--that's a pleasant surprise in itself. [B plus] (Steve Lewis)

Jonathan Valin. **Day of Wrath.** Congdon & Lattes, 1982, 244 pp., $12.95.

Private eye Harry Stoner's latest case is, on the face of it, a simple, straight-forward one. A runaway girl, apparently too old for her years, has disappeared.

Stoner has seen her home and the street on which she lived, and it is all too obvious what she is running from, and what it is she is hoping to find: freedom. Escape from the stifling confinement of middle-class conventionality.

Her boyfriend, the last person to have seen her and the one Stoner suspects helped her on her way, is dead. He has been brutally tortured, his body smashed and broken. If freedom is paradise, Stoner realizes, there is a serpent of evil loose in the garden.

Before he is done, Stoner does himself physical harm, perhaps permanently. His task as he sees it is to rescue the girl—who may not want rescuing--and, in doing so, to reclaim his own sense of values--having rejected for himself the lies the girl's mother lives by--and to redeem, if he can, the romantic ideals of the boy who died.

As I said, straight-forward. Plunging on. No turning back. Valin doesn't believe in doing anything halfway, even when Stoner's cases are as "easy" as this. Overall, it's not the best of the four novels he's written so far, but his views on the malevolent side-effects of massive doses of self-indulgence will chill you--at least a little. [B plus] (Steve Lewis)

E.F. Cunningham. **The Case of the Kidnapped Angel.** Delacorte Press, 1982, 180 pp.

This is the sixth mystery concerning Masao Masuto, Beverly Hills' answer to Charlie Chan. Masuto, an American-born Japanese, is a practicing Buddhist and an intuitive detective. His partner, Sy Beckman, proves, as usual, to be an admirable foil for Masuto, as they investigate the kidnapping of beautiful Angel Barton.

The kidnapping (which proves to be nothing of the kind) is only the first link in this seemingly senseless chain of crimes. Kidnapping leads to murder, and murder begets more murder. By the time that Masuto has played out his hunch, he has succeeded in angering his captain and sufficiently annoying several influential residents to get the city manager on the department's back. But he has also discovered the culprits. This he finds to be somewhat personally rewarding, as he feels that he could have prevented one of the murders.

Unfortunately, Masuto is unable to get enough hard evidence to convict all of the murders, but because this case has more convolutions than U.S. Route 1, we can excuse him.

Cunningham writes in a straight-ahead manner,. His main device in making Masuto a living, breathing character is the constant contrast between Masuto's Zen upbringing of peaceful family life and the insanity of violent death which surrounds him in his occupation.

Another solid effort by E.V. Cunningham. (Alan S. Mosier)

Marvin Kaye. **The Soap Opera Slaughters.** Doubleday, 1982, 183 pp.

Hats off, gentlemen! Archie Goodwin is alive and well, and working under an assumed name. Marvin Kaye's wisecracking detective is as classic a parody of Rex Stout's gumshoe as I've yet encountered.

But there's more! The book is well written and funny in its view of "daytime drama." Kaye has built well upon the strong foundation laid in previous Hilary Quayle books (**The Laurel and Hardy Murders, Bullets for Macbeth**), and the result is a combination of articulate humor and light mystery.

The Soap Opera Slaughters is very reminiscent of Simon Brett's **Situation Tragedy** in its inside view of a television production, but, where Brett is lambasting the venerable BBC, Kay has targeted one of the major networks in our own country. But here the similarities come to an end. This tale is packed with petty rivalries between the actors, production staff, and anyone else within shouting distance.

Hilary is not strongly present in this story (outside of being in Gene's thoughts twenty-four hours a day), but her look-alike cousin, a soap actress, gets Gene entangled in an investigation when cries of murder are heard following the plunge of the head writer from the studio rooftop.

Author Kaye has also tossed in a few inside jokes (a soap character named Ellis Peters, for example) to create an enjoyable, informative mystery and a must for sufferers of "afternoon addiction." (Alan S. Mosier)

Lawrence Block. **A Stab in the Dark.** Arbor House, 1981, 192 pp.

Matt Scudder: ex-cop, alcoholic, erstwhile private eye—no license, but he does what he can.

Nine years after a series of killings known as the Icepick Slayings, the certified nut responsible for them is caught. The father of one of the victims doesn't believe his daughter was killed by the nut and hires Scudder to find out who really did it.

The dust jacket says "a novel of suspense" and means it. A well-drawn plot, very believable characters, and beautifully written. Highly recommended. (Linda Toole)

Lawrence Treat. **Crime and Puzzlement 2.** David R. Godine, 1982, 76 pp., soft cover $5.95.

Again Mr. Treat has given us "solve-them-yourself" mysteries, each complete with picture, brief description, and several questions that may help solve the problem. Solutions are given at the end of the book.

If you missed **Crime and Puzzlement**, this is worth a look as a novelty, but the second time around the gimmick wears a bit thin. (Linda Toole)

Anthony Marriott. **Public Eye: Marker Calls the Tune.** Fontana, 1968.

Some time ago I reviewed Audley Southcott's **Cross That Palm When I Come to It**, a TV spin-off paperback original about seedy, down-at-the-heels private eye Frank Marker. A friend of mine mentioned that he thought that there had been at least one more about Marker—and here it is. Different author, different publisher, much earlier and, in my experience, probably the hardest TV spin-off British mystery book to find. ("Hawkeye" Meyerson spotted this copy on a joint book-hunting trip.)

And the book itself? It's all about Marker's dogged and at times almost self-destructive endeavours to bring to justice an unsavoury crook called Marginar, a man with more angles than Pythagoras. Marker is threatened, beaten up, frightened—but this just makes him more persistent. Plenty of action and plot movement. Well written, and London low-life scenes well depicted. Success for Marker—but also inevitable ultimate failure. (Bob Adey)

Frank Gruber. **Murder '97**. Barker, 1956.

The third in the series (and the first I've read) about grouchy bibliophile P.I. Simon Lash. I'd only bought it to pass on to someone else but read the opening plot synopsis and was hooked. And why not? A client brings in an old boys' book bearing a contemporary inscription and agrees to pay Lash $1,000 (in 1947) to establish to whom the inscription relates. Well, haven't we all wandered from time to time? The big question for Lash is why, of course, the client should be prepared to pay (and, as it emerges, who is he, anyway?), and we're immediately off on a fast-moving, logically-stepped chase by Lash as one contact leads back to another, and another—and so on. Plenty of action, lots of twists and turns, satisfactory conclusion. Lash is definitely the book-collector's private eye. (Bob Adey)

Milton Shulman. **Kill 3**. Collins, 1967.

The author is one of my favorite radio personalities, a Canadian, well known for his mild manner and gentle wit. A surprise to me then that this is a bleak little story of the kidnapping (and subsequent fate) of three working-class children, by a young couple entirely devoid of the milk of human kindness. The twist is that the couple hold out the hostages for a ransom to be paid, not by their penniless widowed mother, but by a firm of well-to-do solicitors. Interesting idea with its germ in a real French case. The whole thing is most effective—and quite chilling. (Bob Adey)

John Wainwright. **Death in a Sleeping City**. Collins, 1965.

A bold first novel by a now prolific author. Wainwright is a former policeman, therefore it is no surprise that the police end of this procedural is handled with an authentic touch. The plot, about a mafia assassination in London, is rather less convincing, and so, to an even greater extent, is the American story that the killers use. The author has done much better since, but this is no mean effort for all that. (Bob Adey)

The Documents In the Case (Letters)

From Michael L. Cook, 3318 Wimberg Ave., Evansville, IN 47712:

While, according to John Nieminski, in the article on my book **Monthly Murders** published in TMF 7:3, the book "as the only work of its kind yet to appear, it is at once indispensible to the serious student," it is flawed by a number of errors in alphabetizing, typing, and several other matters. At least he does not claim any errors in spelling. Kindly advise Mr. Nieminski that "indispensible" is spelled wrong in his article, and should be "indispensable." [**Either spelling is correct, according to** Webster's Third New International Dictionary.]

Nieminski's analysis of the book is certainly flawed in itself, by claiming (unsupported) to have taken a random sampling of 10% of the contents, and then multiplying what he claims as errors by 10, to reach an astronomical figure. His extrapolation would most certainly stretch the credibility; perhaps he has missed his calling and should be working for one of the national pollsters (at least one of which still insists that Dewey beat Truman for President).

My book needs no excuses; it will stand on its own merit. However, excuses are needed for persons who nitpick, and I am sorry and surprised to see John Nieminski join their ranks.

[I am curious—by what number other than 10 should John have multiplied his 10% sample?]

From Joe R. Christopher, English Department, Tarleton State University, Stephenville, TX 76402:

I see that Melinda Reynolds is denigrating my beloved Dorothy L. Sayers in her letter. Are you interested in this paper in which I make clear what I think is the literary complexity of Sayers in what I believe to be one of her two greatest novels (the other is **Gaudy Night**)? [**Of course I am; see elsewhere in this issue.**] It's not a direct answer to Reynolds, of course—no one can dispute matters of taste on a logical basis—but it may suggest why some of us return to Sayers time after time, finding in her a complexity beyond most detective story writers. [...]

I'm not about to dispute all of Reynolds' statements. I don't find myself returning to reread Ngaio Marsh very often, although I try to enjoy her books every so often. I am rather fond of P.D. James, but I agree that most of her mysteries are flat compared to **Innocent**

Blood. (I meant to write a paper this spring on that book—James's one straight novel so far—but I didn't get to it. If I ever get it done, it will go to a meeting for reading before I submit it anywhere for publication.) I remember Josephine Tey's books as nicely done, but it's been over fifteen years since I've read one. On Margery Allingham, I wish Reynolds would try one or two more before she gives up. Allingham changes a goodly amount from book to book. My favorite is **Tiger in the Smoke**, which is not really a detective story—rather, a study of evil—and Campion is of minor importance; if one reads it as a detective story, he or she will condemn it roundly. But I'd call it Allingham's best. I'm not sure about Agatha Christie. I find myself rereading her short stories, but not (very often) her mystery novels. Again, I'm very fond of one of her novels published under the Mary Westmacott by-line, **Absent in the Spring** (I taught it in a graduate class once); it's not a mystery, of course, but it's a lovely minor novel built on irony.

When I reread the above paragraph, I sound like a typical English teacher who doesn't really like mysteries. Let me add that the mystery writer I think I reread most often is Rex Stout. I've written a batch of essays on Ellery Queen and a few on Anthony Boucher, but it's Stout—about whom I have written little and find I have little to say—that I (currently) enjoy the most. (That doesn't apply to new readings; I suppose I read a dozen or so new mysteries per year and enjoy most of them. I **did** write some sort of note on Nero Wolfe's birthplace for **The Baker Street Journal** about eighteen years ago, but I stopped subscribing and my note was never published.)

From Kay Seraphine, 509 17th Street, Huntington Beach, CA 92648:

Would you please add the address and send this note on to Paul Bishop. I am interested in "The Sport of Sleuths" but don't know where to write. [Ouch! Kay wasn't the only one who had to write to Paul care of me, since I neglected to give his address, which is: 31 Tahquitz Dr., Camarillo, CA 93010. I also neglected to give Tom Johnson's address; those of you interested in Tom's Echoes can reach him at 504 E. Morris St., Seymour, TX 76380.

As for a TMF price rise, with the way my utilities are skyrocketing, what's another $3.00 for something I enjoy? (May have to read it by day if I can't afford to turn on the lights!)

From Richard S. Callaghan, Jr., "Oakland," Ivy, VA 22945:

I think TMF is a great read. Your mix and selection of a personal letter from you to your readers, articles, reviews and letters from your readers show a fine editorial hand. [**Aw, shucks** ...]

Accordingly, I cannot offer a suggestion on how TMF could be objectively improved. I can only tell you what one reader would like to see included in your copy.

I would like to read listings of readers' all-time favorite genre books in order of preference. It is not only interesting what a knowledgeable person thinks best, but a great source from which to find future books to read. If reader X submits a list of say his ten to twenty favorites and on the list are a few of one's own favorites, then what has not been read on the list might well be worth hunting down.

Furthermore, what better way to stir up admiration and outrage--the life blood of fanzinedom.

I would propose a contest and offer to put up the prize. Readers could be invited to submit for publication ten, thirteen, twenty (you decide the number, Guy) of their personal favorites in their own order of preference by a certain date. Give each entrant up to five words to keynote each title. For example, he might want to state as to his number one pick "Agatha best--Agatha's best book" and as to another "great literature, desert island quality," and so on.

How could anyone reasonably decide who deserved the prize? The answer is simple, of course, he couldn't. But we wouldn't let this stop us, because the prize would not be for the quality of the effort, but for the effort itself.

All we would need is a "judge" who has no known taste. [Observe, God, that I let that one lie; that kind of restraint has got to count for something, hasn't it?] Don't worry, Guy, I'm not about to suggest you. If we select a judge known to the entrants, we run the risk that some list might be submitted geared to the judge's taste.

How about making the "judge" the pick of the hat. Put the published submissions in your best topper, trot down to your local library, and ask your honest-looking librarian (who ever saw a librarian who didn't look honest?) to pick the winner out.

I'll give a free TMF one-year subscription--not to the winner (you already have this sucker hooked, Guy), but to the library the winner designates. The gift would be made in the name of the winner.

[Alas, Rick, I think you grossly over estimate the willingness of TMFers to indulge in list-making. Years ago I appealed to the readers at large for their choices for ten indispensable secondary sources in our field. I was prepared to work nights compiling the flood of responses into some meaningful order, confident that the result would be of immeasurable use to mystery fans the world over, but only two or three folks bothered to send any sort of response at all. I doubt that the response to your scheme would be much greater, though I will be delighted to run, as letters, any such lists that you folks out there may wish to send in.]

From Martha Alderson, 631 McKinley Ave., Kirkwood, MO 63122:

Enclosed is one review, for David Carkeet's **Double Negative**. I know you have published a review of it before, but I think it's worth calling attention to again. [**Thanks. I've no objection to publishing multiple reviews of books.**] I wanted to like the book even more than I did, given his St. Louis home and the Indiana setting, as well as the linguistics content. I do hope Carkeet is about to publish a second mystery, but I haven't read anything about it. Do you know? [**Not me. Anyone?**]

Are you considering asking for submissions on diskettes? [**Any day now.**] All of this new technology is frightening and exciting!

From Bob Randisi, 1811 East 35th St., Brooklyn, NY 11234:

In response to Greg Goode's letter in 7:3, I'm glad Greg enjoyed the issue, but I'd like to point out that in my letter in a previous issue, to which he alluded, I did not speak out against TMF in general; I merely pointed out that one particular issue did not entirely satisfy me. I have said the same thing in the past as regards TAD, which is not to mean that I do not like TAD in general. I thoroughly enjoy TMF—most of the time. There are those odd issues, however, where there is more to dislike than like, in the way of articles. As usual—and as was the case with 7:3—I enjoy the letters immensely, and the reviews, and the regular columns.

To Jon Breen, who commented on my list of top ten private eyes, I don't believe that I said it was a list of the Best, but of my Favorites. If indeed I did say Best, it was an error on my part. (I don't have an issue of 7:2 at hand, but mean to get one from the Mysterious Bookshop and check this out.) [**What you said was: "I'd like to offer a top ten P.I. list of my own ...."**]

To Teri White: modesty prevented you from including your own name on your list of readable female writers, so allow me to add it. For those who don't know, Teri won the Edgar award this year for Best Paperback with her first novel, **Triangle**. The lady can write.

Glad to see that you (Guy) are touting the Kaypro. I have plans to buy the Kaypro 10, myself. [**If I didn't already have this Kaypro II, I'd buy a Kaypro 10, too. For the rest of you folks, instead of two disk drives, the 10 has a hard disk with storage in the millions of characters plus a double-density floppy disk with a storage of about 400,000. And it only costs a thousand more than the Kaypro II. This is an incredible bargain, folks, and if you are in the market for a computer you owe it to yourselves to look at the Kaypro line—II, IV, or 10, they are all super machines.**]

From Alan S. Mosier, 10 Kathy Lane, Wakefield, MA 01880:

My thanks to Jon L. Breen and Frank Denton for clearing up the mystery of the two John Gardners! I'm sure our "Moriarty Gardner" will be glad to know that he is still alive and well. But, after all, the mistake did somehow belong to the article, actually. Remember the title? "Deduction in Duplicate"!

As per usual, enjoyed Brad Foster's cover. Does this mean that he has taken the suggestion of Greg Goode and is doing some detective covers? If so, might I suggest Basil Rathbone and Nigel Bruce as suitable models?

Speaking of Greg Goode, pass on the information that the second of Frank Thomas's pastiches deals with Chu San Fu as well (**The Sacred Sword**).

Regarding your course of action in the matter of "to raise, or not to raise".... I vote for a retention of present rates. You seem to have no end of enthusiastic contributors that send along reviews and articles just for the fun of it (myself included). However, if I am out-voted, please forward all checks to the above address.

From Randy Himmel, 2107 River Road, Reading, PA 19605:

No. I do not think you should raise the subscription rates to TMF. If you want to pay the contributors, I think it should be tied directly to circulation rate. As you had originally planned it. If circulation warrants it, pay them. Otherwise, don't pay them.

When and if payment to contributors comes about, I think it should only go to people writing articles and columns. Book reviews are just too easy to do. Even the most complicated of them.

You will probably have some people saying, "Yes, raise the rates." These are die-hards and will stick with you till the end. Unfortunately, they are too few. The ones you'll have to worry about are the ones who don't respond to your question. If the rates go up, they will just very silently, but deadly, not resubscribe. And your subscription will dwindle further. [...]

Nieminski and Sampson are top non-fiction writers. Try and encourage them to submit more material.

Your editor's note on buying your computer was very informative. I'm sure it will be very helpful to others when they go to buy a computer.

From Beth Polk, c/o LaGrange Motel, #16, McDonnell Rd., Pleasant Valley, NY 12569:

I'm all in favor of paying something to the people who make publications like TMF possible, even if it does mean a rise in subscription rates. Even though the articles, checklists, etc. would never be done without the love of digging out the information and sharing it, some payment other than our applause seems in order from those of us who just sit back and soak up the benefits.

My thanks to all of them and to you for bringing it all to us.

From Paulette Greene, 140 Princeton Rd., Rockville Centre, NY 11570:

Here we are, in the middle of the longest, hottest spell of hot, hot and humid weather, and you pose the problem of raising the price of TMF. Well of course it is worth it, although I do have a dread of creeping rising prices. However I do have a question: Is half a cent per really worth all the "to do"? My goodness, the articles that appear in TMF reflect hours of scholarly research ... would that I could locate a cataloguer for half a cent per....

But everyone wants to be rewarded. It is only natural. Is it possible to have a vote at the end of the year for the best article, and present an award, thus? Have readers vote on it? Then use the rise in price for some kind of award--the special TMF award pen.... (Had to thrown in my ¢ cent's worth of advice, too!!)

Back to business. Want to tell you how much I have enjoyed reading about your computer experiences. Me--never. I can barely type, and I am just waiting for someone to get a home computer who will do it for me, as I now have catalogue typed by crackerjack outside typist. This way I can make all changes on master copy and then send it off for fine typing.

From Fred Isaac, 1501 Milvia St., Berkeley, CA 94709:

[You folks think you've had trouble with the Postal Service? Then consider the case of poor Fred Isaac--he didn't receive 7:1, 7:2, or 7:3, all of which were sent to the correct address. He wrote to ask me what was the problem, and, not having seen 7:2 in which his earlier letter was printed, he said a few new words about some matters he discussed in that letter. Here they are:]

I went to a conference hosted by the University of the Pacific in Stockton in February at which one of the sessions was on library materials regarding the mystery. The audience was mostly fans and not many intellectuals, or academics, or even pretend-experts (as I am, or think I am). At any rate, the women running the group were down on the journals, and only mildly approved of TAD. But they sneered at TMF, for reasons I have yet to fathom. I got very irate, and am still. The fact that there are so few serious magazines keeps us in secondary status as far as critics are concerned. Grrrrr!

Oh, yes. I gave what I thought was a useful talk at the Popular Culture meeting in Kansas, on the lack of communication between pure fans and critics who began as fans. It will need a good deal of work, but if you're interested I will gladly do it and send it on to you. [By all means, do so.]

From Ev Bleiler, still at large somewhere in New Jersey:

You certainly pushed the right button with your comments about the Drood article in the **Harvard Magazine**. The article doesn't deserve such publicity, and this must really be the silly season if newspaper columnists are picking it up.

The article was pretty bad. The fellow who wrote it had a bright idea and then wrote it up in a gosh-wow manner, but obviously he hadn't read **Drood** thoroughly and knew nothing about **Drood** scholarship. It is riddled with mistakes, and once these are corrected there is little more resemblance between **Drood** and Webster-Parkman than between any two murders.

I wrote the enclosed letter and sent it off. After a month, I got a little note from a sub-editor saying, in effect, "My, we didn't know that people read Dickens that closely" and closing with a vague statement that my letter might be published. Well, my letter wasn't published, but the **Harvard Magazine** did publish a serious, solemn letter praising the article.

As I've discovered before, the **Harvard Magazine** does not like to be caught in error. When I was in college, we used to be told, "You can always tell a Harvard man, but you can't tell him anything."

So, here's a xerox of the letter. If you have any use for it, fine; if not, throw it away.

[Here follows Ev's letter, dated 7 January 1983:]

Dear Sir:

Your recent article on **The Mystery of Edwin Drood** was thought-provoking, if not convincing. But it contained too many careless mistakes.

Page 45: Dickens did not begin "the first of his monthly installments" in April 1870. Forster records that Dickens read the first installment at Forster's home on October 26, 1869.
Page 45: There is no textual basis for the statement that Drood "entered one of the ancient buildings near an English cathedral." Drood may have entered the cathedral, or he may have died outside. The text does not say.
Page 47: There is no direct textual evidence for the statement that

Jasper was a "dabbler in animal magnetism"—which, by the way, was not the same thing as hypnotism. The suggestion of animal magnetism is a modern interpretation of events, and may or not be correct.

Page 47: Drood's watch was not found in the river. It was found on Cloisterham Weird, and the suggestion is that it was never in the water.

Page 47: Jasper did not steal a key to a sarcophagus. The key was to the Sapsea crypt.

Page 48: Dickens did not tell Luke Fildes that Drood would be strangled with a scarf. Fildes is very clear that the "weapon" was a long necktie.

Page 48: And this is a bad error. The statement that Dickens revealed the general plot of **Drood** to Forster in a letter is not correct. No such letter has ever been found, and Forster saved everything from Dickens. If Dickens had written such a letter, there would have been no argument about what happens in **Drood**. Nor did Dickens, even orally, say that the body would be dissolved in quicklime. Indeed, some modern scholars have argued that Dickens knew that quicklime would preserve the body, not destroy it.

Page 48: Another bad error. Charles Dickens, Jr., did not write a continuation to **Drood**. There is a book, **John Jasper's Secret**, which unscrupulous American publishers have reissued under the names of Charles Dickens, Jr., and Wilkie Collins. But it is common knowledge that it was written by Henry Morford, an American Journalist.

On this level of accuracy in small details, one might say that in Jonson's **Hamlet** Prince Hamlet, after attending Ophelia's wedding feast, commits suicide with a tomahawk.

From Jeff Banks, Box 13007 SFA Sta., Nacogdoches, TX 75962:

About your increase in sub rates: Do it! You'll probably remember I urged you to over a year ago.

About your plans to pay contributors: I don't approve. We are all egotists, and contributions to TMF are (and should be, unless and until you do achieve a vast readership) labors of love. Your much vaster investment of time and effort should (and I believe will) inspire willing imitation.

I am ready to write for free (not even contributor copies) so long as you keep publishing. Yes, I know I've been a much less frequent contributor of late; but I will do better.

From Geoff Bradley, 9 Vicarage Hill, South Benfleet, Essex, SS7 1PA, ENGLAND:

I would, of course, renew my subscription in the face of a $3.00 increase; indeed, if necessary, I would pay more. However, I think I must come down against payment for articles. It seems to me that one of the virtues of your magazine is that the articles, written as they are for the love of it, reflect the sheer enjoyment of the writers concerned. At present, writers have no incentive other than the love of the game. I think that's how I prefer it.

Having said that, I am in favour of your raising subscriptions to their optimum level for the greatest income (or least expense) to yourself. I can never read your comments on the finances of running such a magazine with a dry eye.

I read your comments on Paul Bishop's Thieftaker Journals with great interest and hurriedly wrote a letter requesting a copy. Only then did I notice that you had given no address. Anyway I have enclosed the letter in the hope that you may be able to forward it.

Finally, with regard to the letter from Don Ireland, if you have not been inundated with similar letters from booksellers the world over I would be grateful if you would mention that I, too, issue catalogues of Detective Fiction for sale.

From William F. Deeck, 9020 Autoville Dr., College Park, MD 20740:

I will vote "yes" on the increase in subscription rate of $3.00. It is, after all, the price—and for how long?—of one inexpensive paperback. Which paperback I will forgo, I don't know, but surely I can do without one over a year's time.

I have no idea whether this would be of interest to anyone, but I was recently browsing through **The Concise Oxford Dictionary of Proverbs** and came across many familiar names as sources of the quotations used to illustrate the proverbs. Some of these were: C. Brand, C. Aird, J. Le Carre, B. Paul, J. Porter, V. Canning, G. Mitchell, A. Price, O. Mills, D. Kyle, A. Christie, R. Thomas, J. Drummond, L. Deighton, E. Lathen, G. Lyall, R. Barnard, F.W. Crofts, D. Francis, D. Sayers, S. Woods, M. Seeley, M. Coles, E. Peters. M. Gilbert, E. Linnington, J. Sturrock (I guess this is J. G. Jeffreys), P. Wentworth, K. Bonfiglioni, A. Gilbert, C. Dickson, L. Maynell, C. Dexter, and N. Marsh.

Roughly twenty percent of the proverbs through D had a quotation from a mystery or suspense writer, and there were some titles that sounded like mysteries but I did not recognize the authors' names.

I wrote to the editor of this particular dictionary, asking about the frequency of these quotations, and this was his response:

> There are several aspects to the question of why mystery and suspense writers are so frequently quoted. One is undoubtedly the taste of my readers. Another leads on from this: if you are searching for proverbs and come across a rich vein, then the tendency is to carry on in that vein at the expense of others. I remember myself despairing of tracking down a modern example of **good men are scarce** until I chanced upon it in John Le Carre's **Smiley's People**. And yet I feel that the proverb really is more common in these sources, which reflect the speech of the people more closely than does much of the work of "serious" fiction. I would, however, prefer to cite a classic author rather than a writer of pulp fiction or a newspaper, and have by no means restricted the reading to crime and spy novels!

From Frank Floyd, Rt. 3, Box 139-F, Berryville, AR 72616:

You asked our opinion concerning a subscription rate increase. My opinion is that **The Mystery Fancier** rates are sufficiently high. But—since you seemingly want so badly to pay contributing authors, I would go along with you on the raise.

As for any money which I might have coming, I would as soon donate it to some project benefitting **The Mystery Fancier** somehow, should other contributors be willing to do likewise in numbers such that a fund could accumulate in a sizeable enough amount for useful employment.

From Evelyn A. Herzog, 235 West 15th St., New York, NY 10011:

Thanks for the light-handed editing on my Kildare piece. [...]
We lost a line in the first footnote, concerning original publication of the Kildare stories. It should read: "... **Dr. Kildare Takes Charge** as **Dr. Kildare Goes Home**, a four-part serial in **Argosy** beginning 1 June 1940; **Dr. Kildare's Crisis** as a four-part serial in **Argosy** beginning 21 December 1940; ...." [Damn! Blew another one.]

[**From a later letter:**]
Though among the ranks of the chronically overdrawn, I can't object very strenuously to a rise in the subscription rate. We're getting the benefit, after all, of that very handsome new computer's work, and that's some business expense. And your own time counts for a lot.

However, I can't see TMF's paying for articles. Your account of the ups and downs of the subscription list ended with your acceptance that your readership would be just us die-hard mystery fans with a taste for lit. crit., rather than a wider audience. So be it. As writers as well as readers, we mostly "play the game for the game's own sake," and I think it is better so. (Though I'm not one of TMF's regular writers, I speak as a veteran reader, writer, and sometime editor in Sherlockiana, a related cottage industry.) As you acknowledge, the payment would necessarily have to be something in the nature of a token—given to honor the writers who have been giving their best efforts all along. Money only complicates things; plough it back in. The opportunity to publish in our field for our own people is payment enough.

From Bob Adey, in the midst of a move, but still in England:

First, TMF 7:2. Marv Lachman found less to like in the Keating-edited critical work **Whodunit** than I did. I haven't checked the biographical section in detail against **Encyclopedia of Mystery and Detection**, but I did take from **Whodunit** names of a goodly number of modern writers (mainly espionage) who were new to me, and not, I think, covered in **Encyclopedia**. These include Rennie Airth, Patrick Alexander, C.A. Haddad, and Kenneth O'Hara, all fairly recent authors so no criticism of **Encyclopedia**. But the point I'm making is that the author biography does cover a lot of new people, most of whom I've found very much to my liking.

I was interested to read George Dove's review of **Tantalizing Locked Room Stories,** having recently read both the new locked-room anthologies. Ed Hoch's provided more balanced fare, but only one story unknown to me (and that specially written for the volume), while Asimov's, though patchy, provided several unusual items outside my previous ken, and in the Woodham story the most original and enjoyable of the lot. Something of a tour de force.

Bob Randisi's list of PIs was fascinating, not least because it contained several writers I know little or nothing about. My own weakness in these matters is for witty dialogue so that my first division would have to include Timothy Harris, Robert B. Parker, Raymond Chandler, Albert Lewin, and P.B. Yuill. Lavin and Kavanaugh would be there too by dint of sheer power of writing, but the overall result is very different from Bob's—which makes it all the more fascinating, doesn't it?

I would be interested to know which authors Melinda Reynolds enjoys—presumably male only. It might be possible to point her in the direction of women authors she might enjoy. Of the ladies dealt with, I personally like Sayers, Tey, and Christie, am uncertain about James, like only a few early Marsh (and those not especially) and can't stand Allingham at any price. Sayers I would accept as an acquired taste, and Christie I know can produce a violent reaction. Could I suggest that if Melinda cares to venture again with Tey she try either **The Daughter of Time**, where Grant's introspection is perhaps excusable [nothing Grant—or Tey, for that matter—does in that book is excusable], or **The Franchise Affair**, which I recall as being non-Grant, and a very good book indeed. I don't imagine for one moment that she was looking for gratuitous advice, but I give it anyway. And what about Hilda Lawrence or Margaret Millar, two more I'd recommend to anyone,—though it is essential to choose the right titles—Lawrence's **Death of a Doll**, or Millar's **The Iron Gates** or **How Like an Angel**.

Next to 7:3. Yes, yes, of course I'll pay the increased rate. Gotta have my fix, and not exactly exorbitant rates after all.

An amazing piece of work from John Nieminski. I shudder to think how long it took. It's a funny thing about proof reading. No matter how careful you are, they slip through (as anyone who has read **Locked Room Murders** will confirm). I think that you read what you expect to see.

Bob Sampson's piece on Anthony Wynne was very welcome as so little has been written about him. Wynne was quite adept at setting up murder situations (usually impossible ones) and explaining them. Unfortunately, in between these was one hell of a lot of padding, and not exactly grade-one quality at that. I can incidentally confirm that Hailey appears in the three books that Bob was uncertain about.

And finally to the most intriguing piece in TMF in many a long day. Townsend's article on "How I Bought My Computer." No, I'm not being sarcastic. I really enjoyed every word of it, despite the fact that I know little about computers and can't begin to imagine how a computer could produce the magazines I have in front of me. Still, thank God they do. Super covers, incidentally.

P.S. I have borrowed from Neville [Wood], for the duration of my stay here, **A Treasury of Victorian Detective Stories** (Harvester Press, 1980), edited by none other than E.F. Bleiler. In the introduction mention is made that "in the 1860s John B. Williams and Andrew Forrester, Jr., each devised sealed rooms ... of some ingenuity." There is a Forrester story in the volume which appears at first sight not to be a locked-room story, and no story at all by Williams. I would be grateful to Mr. Bleiler if he could provide the relevant details either directly or through these columns, as I have frankly not previously run across either story.

From Jiro Kimura, 2-10-11 Shimo-ochiai, #A-202, Shinjuku-ku, Tokyo, JAPAN:

It's very sad to hear Jud Sapp is dead. When Paul Bishop's Thieftaker Journals had one of its issues dedicated to the memory of Jud Sapp, I thought it must have been another guy by the name of Jud Sapp. Now that you wrote about him, I felt moved.

Jud was a nice fella. He bought a copy of my picture book and thanked me for publishing it before I thanked him for buying it. After one of the Wolfe Pack dinners, he invited all the members to his hotel suite, where we had a nice good time, and he was always a nice considerate host.

When he asked me in a letter to send him photographs I took at one of the Wolfe Pack meetings, I didn't send him any photos. My excuse was that my photo files were, and still are, disorganized after we moved from New York to Tokyo. Another excuse: I don't usually send photos to single persons for their personal use unless I take their pictures or unless they publish some newsletters or periodicals for others. I was burned once when one of the Wolfe Pack **Gazette** editorial staff didn't do anything about my photos I had sent.

Anyway, I didn't send any photos to Jud. Now I feel terribly bad about it. Sorry, Jud. But this apology is too late.

From Mike Nevins, 7045 Cornell, University City, MO 63130:

Thanks for another excellent TMF. John Nieminski's "Closing the Gap" is a classic. I don't recall ever seeing such an in-depth analysis of what is right and wrong with a mystery reference work.

On the burning issue of the moment, whether you should raise your subscription price and pay your contributors half a cent a word, speaking for myself I'd prefer to see the prices stay where they are and myself and the other contributors unpaid. But keep in mind that I'm biased, since the **Globe-Democrat** pays me a whopping $27.50 per review anyway.

Frank Denton asked (p. 43) about other movies based on Desmond Bagley novels. **The Mackintosh Man** (1973), starring Paul Newman and James Mason and directed by John Huston, was nominally based on Bagley's 1971 novel, **The Freedom Trap.** I paid to see the movie when it first came out. Waste of money. Bagley incidentally was almost the spitting image of Fred Dannay. I remember seeing Bagley across a crowded room at an MWA function once and telling the person I was with that it was Fred. If only it were still possible to make that mistake again!

Jon Breen isn't quite right in saying that Brett Halliday "became a house name" in the final years of the Mike Shayne saga. The last few Torquil hardcovers and all of the Dell paperbacks about Shayne were all written by one man, Robert Terrall, who also used the by-lines John Gonzales and Robert Kyle. The Shayne magazine stories of course **were** written by various hands. The best of those done by Dennis Lynds in the sixties (and he cranked out the vast majority of the MSMM novelets during that decade) are better, as far as I'm concerned, than most of Halliday's genuine Shaynes.

Myrtis Broset, 204 S. Spalding St., Spring Valley, IL 61362:

I will pay the $15.00, but I need a written guarantee, with your signature certified to by a notary public, attesting to the fact that you will keep on publishing **The Mystery Fancier** for another year. Golly gee, with a whole $56.45 profit on every issue, you are planning to fly away to some far-away island, no doubt, and will leave us poor fans without "The Fancier." We will all be poorer, won't we? Three dollars' worth!

We lost another mystery author when Ross Macdonald passed away. His memory will live on in Lew Archer.

Anyone who buys the reprints of Cornell Woolrich's books finds an introduction by Francis M. Nevins telling a little of Woolrich's life. I recently found a copy of **Nightwebs**, edited by Francis M. Nevins, which is filled with short stories, all by Woolrich. Most of them I hadn't read before and so was happy to find this treasure. Since I like to read about the author whose book I am reading, I was delighted with the 22-page introduction on the life of Woolrich. In the back of the book is a checklist on all Woolrich's works. It is a treasure indeed.

I read somewhere that Mr. Nevins is doing another book on Woolrich's stories. I hope it's true. I'm looking forward to it.

From James R. Callen, 4707 Falcon St., Rockville, MD 20853:

First, I vote Yes on your proposed price increase. You're doing a fine job--keep it up.

Second, I would like to voice my opinion on Melinda Reynolds' letter on women mystery writers. First, I have read thousands of mysteries, starting in the early 1930s, and I have never "given up" after fifty pages or a few paragraphs (as Melinda Reynolds states she has) on any mystery--be it by male or female writer. Sure, some of them turned out to be pretty bad, but I would at least give the writer his/her due by finishing the book. Incidentally, as many if not more of these bad books were by males. Philo Vance was as big a "silly-ass" as Lord Peter Wimsey. I found P.D. James's **Death of an Expert Witness** to be an excellent book. I won't comment on her attack on Agatha Christie, the Queen of Mystery Writers. I honestly don't believe that Melinda Reynolds is a mystery fan. What's her objection to Dell Shannon, whose police procedurals will stand up with anyone's? Has she read any Patricia Highsmith, any June Thomson?

Is the Teri White who agreed with Melinda Reynolds' letter the Teri White who wrote the recent Edgar-winner, **Triangle**? If she is, I wonder if Melinda has read her book and if she liked it. I have read it and recommend it to all TMF fans.

From Ben Fisher, Box 816, University, MS 38677:

First, the special Poe issue of **University of Mississippi Studies in English**, edited by yours truly, is out, may have items of value for TMF readers, and is available for $5.00 from the Business Manager,

UMSE, English Department, Ole Miss, University, MS 38677. The issue to follow, available some time in early 1984 (I doubt sooner), will publish for the first time a play—one-act—based on Ernest Bramah's **Tragedy at Brookbend Cottage**, together with an introduction by William White.

Please remember to remind readers to send me items for listing in my "Fugitive Poe References: A Bibliography," for items haven't been exactly pouring in (fear not; I've dredged up plenty on my own, but I don't want anyone who has something good to say about Edgar in writings not immediately revelatory of that fact getting disappointed because they are left out). I also remind folks that the Poe Studies Association, of which I'm president, always welcomes members, at $5.00 a year, for which they get a semi-annual **Newsletter** and can attend meetings held during the annual MLA conventions; and that The Edgar Allan Poe Society welcomes members for $2.00 annually or $25.00 for life membership--for which they receive the published annual lecture(s) free.

I have two collections of edited essays forthcoming from the Poe Society: **Poe and Our Times** (essays on his impact on the twentieth century), 1983 [not yet completed]; and **Poe and His Times** (essays on influences on Poe and about his influences on later nineteenth-century writers/artists), due out next year. Both books will run writings about Poe and mystery/detective fiction.

My work on John Dickson Carr progresses slowly just now, although I would be delighted to have sent to me items relevant to a book mainly critical/analytical, but with at least a chapter on biography, to me at my Box 816 address. Acknowledgements will come in due course.

Finally, too, I have turned up the last pieces in the puzzle of Frederick Irving Anderson bibliography, so far as locating his stories in original appearances goes, so sometime during this year I hope to put that in shape for publication. I've found that chasing down Anderson or things about him is almost like living out a detective story, with every false clue/hope pretty much dashed!

From Teri White, 3280 Landsmere, Shaker Hts., OH 44122:

After my longish letter last time, just some brief comments:
1. I support the price increase.
2. I very much enjoyed Martha Alderson's essay on the gay PIs. There might be some significance in the fact that the piece was written by a female. Also, just as an added note to the books she mentioned, I would suggest **Death Trick** by Richard Stevenson. His hero, Don Strachey, seems to find a middle ground somewhere between Valentine and Brandstetter--not as jolly as the first nor as gloomy as the second. Also, just to be fair, let me mention a book called **Lamar Ransom, Private Eye**, by David Galloway. Set in old time L.A., it features a lesbian detective.
3. Finally (and I seem to have gone on longer than intended) I enjoyed reading about your adventures in word processing—especially since as I read it, I am awaiting the delivery of my own Kaypro IV, which is much the same as the II, except with more storage capacity. After months of looking, judging, and trying to decide, it was very nice to find some confirmation that I made the right choice.

From Andy Jaysnovitch, 6 Dana Estates Dr., Parlin, NJ 08859:

Well, I finally knocked out another issue of **The Not So Private Eye**. I can't help but wonder how you can put out TMF on such a regular schedule. [**This is regular!?**] Even if we forget about the typing, which you probably do three times as fast as I do, there is still the million other chores that must be done before you can finally stuff them envelopes.

Before I forget, I don't think that you should get into paying for articles, etc. If anything, put that money into promotion. And if you ever make a nickle profit somewhere along the line, keep it!

Starting with my very next issue, I'm going to make a **real** drastic change with TNSPE. I'm going to the newsletter format. TNSPE will become primarily a news and reviews zine, with one or maybe two normal size issues similar to TMF a year. The rest will be newsletters.

I hope to have the first newsletter TNSPE ready for distribution at the Bouchercon. Hope to see you there.

If you have any space in the next TMF, I'd appreciate a mention of TNSPE #11. It'll be a lot easier to promote a newsletter since I can **give away** most of the print run, but until then I need some help.

Contents of #11 are: "Dicks and Janes," a look at the way pulpsters described the dames in their Eye's life. In "Five Eyes" we compare five current private-eye series, Max Collins takes an in-depth look at the recent **I, the Jury** movie, also an article on the hardboiled Hemingway, plus news and reviews. Forty-four pages for $2.00 first-class ($3 foreign). [**Andy forgot to mention that the issue has a Brad Foster cover as well.**]

From Linda Toole, 40 Hermitage Rd., Rochester, NY 14617:

Thank you for your lovely and touching encomium to Jud Sapp. My hurt is miniscule compared to Linda's, but I still feel a loss; it helps to know someone shares it.

Rack up another vote for a Brad Foster **Spicy Detective** cover. I'd love to see what he could do along this line.

The reason you haven't received a copy of **The Gazette**, volume 2, #1, is that you sent in a renewal form. 2/1 was automatically sent to those who already belonged, in hopes that they would re-up (and probably as a partial apology for being so late). The powers that be probably think you already have your copy. [...] [**Yeah, everything finally came, a mere three years after my initial inquiry.**]

I see that I did not make myself clear. What I **meant** to say was that Bob Sampson should write fiction.

Thank you, Melinda, for elucidating your/our/my feelings about women mystery writers. I concur completely with all your points and am glad you wrote it, because I think you did a better job than I could have (heck, I know you did). The first mysteries I ever read were Nancy Drew books, which I enjoyed. My brother introduced me to Sherlock Holmes and Nero Wolfe, after which I was on my own. I know I read some Christie and Sayers, but maybe not their best. I feel the same as you do about their books. I did manage to read **The Murder of Roger Ackroyd,** and did enjoy it, but I think I persevered only because I had read so much in praise of it.

I can recommend one woman author. Lucille Kallen's C.B.

Greenfield books are well worth reading. They are somewhat reminiscent of Stout, and are bright, intelligent, and interesting. Above all, they have a sense of humor (without being humor books), a quality all too often lacking in writing of any kind.

Regarding Greg Goode's comment on Nevil Shute, I still stand pat. As far as I'm concerned, the operative words in TCCMW are CRIME and MYSTERY. Granted, nuclear war is a moral crime, but I would prefer that TCCMW concentrate on more traditional crimes--murder, theft, blackmail, etc.--and mysteries (locked room, for example). That is why I object to Shutes' inclusion.

[**Another letter:**]

Re payment for articles: I'm ambivalent, basically because (as happened in the pulps) I'm afraid of padding. Also, there are some regular contributors now (i.e. Jane Bakerman) whose style is already overly verbose (especially as compared to Bob Adey). Would you edit out the extraneous? [**No more than I already do.**] Then again, how much can be edited out without sacrificing individuality? Like I said, I'm ambivalent.

From Greg Goode, 50 Washburn Park, Rochester, NY 14620:

By the time this letter appears, I will be at the above address. I received TMF 7:3 shortly before I left Germany and intended to save it for the various planes, trains, buses, and boats I intended to travel with, but temptation got the better of me and I read it cover to cover the day I got it.

Was most impressed by John Nieminski's article on **Monthly Murders**. The only negative comment I can make is an insignificant non-genre related one. The misplaced terminal letter in Mr. Cook's rendering of Avram Davidson's "The Liberty of the Subject" is the y. This letter by itself is neither a vowel nor a consonant, but is defined phonetically according to its use. In "liberty" it functions as a vowel, not a consonant. But surel that does not mattery, for Mr. Nieminski's article is a model of painstaking research of the sort many index compilers might justifiably fear might be directed towards their work. And the ability to check entries against 265 issues, 28 titles, is no mean feat of collecting.

Martha Alderson's "Deadly Edges" was a balanced, sensible, interesting account, and I appreciate the annotations in the author bibliographies.

From Gene Christie, Box 658, Conyers, GA 30207:

The current volume is my first of TMF and I certainly feel like a newcomer reading the letters from long-time subscribers. But I will be brash enough to suggest that Joe Christopher give Cornell Woolrich another chance. He states in 7:2 that he tried "Jane Brown's Body," found it poorly written, and never tried C.W. again. Personally, I greatly enjoyed this story, although I came to it late in my reading of Woolrich. Come on, Joe, try Cornell again, maybe one of the "black" novels. You don't know what you're missing!

From Kevin Barbero, Murder by the Book, 4 Market St., West Warwick, RI 02893:

I think your subscribers would be interested in my catalog. [...] I have approximately 15,000 books in stock, ranging from fine first editions to reading copies. Since I've been interested in collectible paperbacks for a few years, I've started listing a paperback section which seems to be gathering new collectors. I also offer a free search service and would be happy to receive any want lists. The catalog is available free upon request.

From Marv Lachman, 34 Yorkshire Dr., Suffern, NY 10901:

Way to go, Bob Randisi. Everyone knows that making lists is next to Godliness. Here's my list of the dozen best Private Eyes, though I am not putting them in any special order:
Raymond Chandler's PHILIP MARLOWE
John Evans' PAUL PINE
Wade Miller's MAX THURSDAY
Fredric Brown's ED & AM HUNTER
Ross Macdonald's LEW ARCHER
Thomas B. Dewey's MAC
William Campbell Gault's BROCK CALLAHAN
Ed Lacy's TOUIE MOORE
Michael Lewin's ALBERT SAMSON
P.D. James's CORDELIA GRAY
Dashiell Hammett's CONTINENTAL OP
Bill Pronzini's "NAMELESS"
We agree on two (Mac and "Nameless"). I'm afraid some of your choices (Tobin, Hardman, and Reddman) wouldn't even make my third dozen. Still, I enjoyed your list and your letter.

[Continued from page 26]
Kubrick's future, should not be consigned to fragmented late-night showings on TV and to filmographies. Kubrick remains a challenging and demanding filmmaker, and we should, perhaps, study the earlier moves in his game before we try to judge too quickly the newer ones.